WORKING WITH
AGING
CLIENTS

WORKING WITH
AGING
CLIENTS

A Guide for Legal, Business, and Financial Professionals

CAROLYN L. ROSENBLATT

Printed in the United States of America.

19 18 17 16 15 5 4 3 2 1

ISBN: 978-1-63425-161-7

e-ISBN: 978-1-63425-162-4

Library of Congress Cataloging-in-Publication Data

Rosenblatt, Carolyn L., author.
  Working with Aging Clients : a guide for attorneys, business, and financial professionals / Carolyn L. Rosenblatt, RN, BSN, attorney.
      pages cm
  Includes bibliographical references and index.
  ISBN 978-1-63425-161-7 (softcover : alk. paper) -- ISBN 978-1-63425-162-4 (e-book) 1. Older people--Legal status, laws, etc.--United States. 2. Attorney and client--United States. I. Title.
  KF390.A4R67 2015
  344.7303'26--dc23   2015015341

Discounts are available for books ordered in bulk. Special consideration is given to state bars, CLE programs, and other bar-related organizations. Inquire at Book Publishing, ABA Publishing, American Bar Association, 321 N. Clark Street, Chicago, Illinois 60654-7598.

www.ShopABA.org

Dedication

A marvelous example of a person who aged well was my beloved grandmother, Louise Blondeau Crum, the first older person I knew. This book is dedicated first to her. "Mimi," as we called her, had her independence for a very long time, during which she was fully engaged with her family, her community, and her church. She protected me, taught me, and showed me thousands of things. She inspired me to pursue nursing, as she had, and for that I thank her to this day. She also taught me that aging can be a positive thing, filled with wisdom. She was my inspiration. I have loved working with elders over the years, no doubt due to her positive influence.

My wise and helpful husband and psychologist-business partner, Dr. Mikol Davis, is another inspiration for this book, so I also dedicate it to him. With his 40 years of experience with individuals and families of all ages, he has provided a rich and valuable perspective on the aging person, family conflicts, and communication that helped me countless times as I wrote. I am ever grateful for his input, his technological skills (which far exceed mine), and his patience. Whenever I was stuck with a frozen computer or any other tech problem, he was the guy to fix it, never complaining.

Finally, I dedicate this to those I call my many teachers. You are my 10,000 or so patients/clients I worked with as a nurse over 10 years and my hundreds of legal clients, consulting clients, and mediation clients. I derived much of the material in this book from helping you with your issues. I thank you for your trust in me. I hope you know that in some way you inspired me to write and help others learn from your experience.

Contents

Preface

How did this book come to be? I have spent decades in contact with elders, and what I have seen—both inside and outside my nursing career—has been a lot of misunderstanding of aging itself. I saw dismissiveness, stereotyping, and assumptions that were not fair to the older person, with both patients and legal clients. I began to write about aging partly out of frustration with that unfairness, and partly because of the inevitable vulnerabilities many elders have to face. I didn't want to see them overlooked, taken advantage of, or treated less than respectfully. I wanted to share what I have learned from thousands of patients and what nearly three decades of practicing law, sometimes representing aging clients, has taught me. I wanted to bring into focus all that I have studied and learned about aging since retiring from a litigation practice to focus on aging clients and their families as a consultant and mediator. I am a senior citizen myself, a Baby Boomer with an aging mother-in-law, and some of what I write about is from personal experience as well as from my professional perspective.

My first career was in nursing. As a student, I had worked as an aide in nursing homes, one of which was across from my college dorm. After graduating from the University of San Francisco with my bachelor's degree in nursing and my public health certification, I spent some time working in hospitals and nursing homes. I then got a job as a home health nurse, visiting clients (both wealthy and low-income) throughout the day. Most had financial worries as they aged. I recall that when I started, the supervisor told me that most of our agency's clients were older people. I wasn't sure I wanted geriatrics for a career; I thought that sounded kind of dull. Wrong! As it turned out, I loved it. My older clients were the most appreciative, it seemed, and we got along quite well. I often noticed how vulnerable they were, because of their many impairments and the need for others in the family to look out for them. Yet, at the same time, most of them wanted fiercely to hold on to any independence they could. I worked at honoring that while also trying to keep them safe.

All those years ago, nursing was not fairly compensated in relation to the extent of nurses' education and the responsibility we had for our clients. (Fortunately, that has changed!) So eventually I chose to go to law school, working my way through while nursing, in an effort to still be of service to individuals while improving my financial prospects. I worked as a lawyer for established firms and eventually opened my own personal injury litigation practice, which succeeded for 25 years until my retirement. During those years, when I represented a 90-year-old, I was appalled at how inconsiderate others appeared to be in failing to accommodate her aging. When somewhat frail elders were my clients, I became ever more protective of their rights than I was for younger persons, mainly because the elders sometimes had trouble speaking up for themselves, but also because an injured older person generally does not recover in the same way a younger person does. The failure of my lawyer brethren to understand this often upset me, and I wondered why they seemed so unaware. I realized that perhaps no one had ever explained the specific problems of aging to them—and I thought about what I could do to change that.

After retiring from my litigation practice, I founded AgingParents.com, a consulting and mediation office, with my psychologist husband, Dr. Mikol Davis. We expanded it to AgingInvestor.com to help educate financial services professionals about aging clients. Our work with aging clients and their adult children has taught both of us a great deal about the problems families have and how to best solve those problems. After hearing hundreds of stories and mediating countless family conflicts over the past several years, I felt it was time to share some of the commonalities and lessons learned. Every client has been my teacher.

I also grew increasingly concerned about elder abuse. I saw lawyers who thought they were being good advocates unwittingly aiding and abetting abuse by taking an impaired elder's word for everything, never questioning obvious signs of memory loss. Perhaps they simply didn't know the danger signs of cognitive impairment well enough to see how complex an issue this is. I wanted to change that too. And I wanted to help not only lawyers, but also business and financial professionals to better recognize the safety risks posed by financial decisions when an elder with incipient dementia was in front of them.

My effort here is from both my nursing perspective, having personally had my hands on thousands of aging clients over 10 years of nursing, and my legal perspective. In combining these two points of view, my hope is that you, the reader, will come away better prepared to address the aging clients who will inevitably cross your path at some point. Whether it is in your office or in your own family, my hope is that your understanding of the aging person/client will deepen. I also hope that you will take special care of these folks, whether family, friends, or clients, in whatever way you provide service to them. After all, they are ourselves, a few years down the road.

Introduction

I have made a special effort to keep this work short and to the point, to allow you to focus on what I think is most important for anyone to know about Working with Aging Clients. While all of us may think we're pretty good at understanding our clients, there may be many hidden truths we need to bring to the surface when our clients become elders.

If you have not specifically studied aging in your professional or business education, your understanding of aging clients will be limited to a small universe of some clients you have known and perhaps the elders in your own family. That lack of experience can narrow your perspective. It can also cause you to stereotype or make unfounded assumptions that can hurt your client. It can cause you to miss important problems that should inform your actions. I hope to broaden your universe of knowledge about elders to include what those in the aging field, the study of gerontology, and health-care practitioners can share that directly applies to our work.

Aging is becoming more and more of an issue of our time, as longevity has increased dramatically over the past 20 years in particular. What this means is that the number of elders among us is growing, and the proportion of aging persons in our society is shifting upward. As a consequence, most—if not all—of us are going to be serving aging clients. It does not matter what specialty we have or what market we work in, nor whether we are lawyers, business advisors, financial professionals, or others. We are now facing or will soon be facing a rising tide of aging folks among us. Some refer to this as "the silver tsunami." Some acknowledge it by simply pointing out that we will soon be seeing more walkers and wheelchairs than baby strollers on the streets.

We live in a youth-obsessed culture where older people are often dismissed or marginalized. In the first chapter, I address myths and stereotypes about aging, in the hope that we can see our own biases better. If we get past the negative mind-set our society thrusts upon us about aging, we are all better off. We can also make smarter decisions, offer better recommendations, and give higher-quality service to our clients when we refrain from making unfounded assumptions about them.

In the second chapter, on challenges, I go through some of the difficulties you can anticipate when Working with Aging Clients. Their sensory impairments, physical limitations, and mobility issues are one part of this. The other big challenge is the cognitive impairment problem; I stress how complex and difficult it can be to understand and address this issue.

The third chapter addresses some of the most common elder-specific issues we see. These include everything from driving and residence choices to loss of financial decision-making ability, financial elder abuse, and caregiving.

The fourth chapter looks at communication with elders. I point out what works best and recommend ways to adapt your communication to your aging client, based on an understanding of effective approaches. My intention in this chapter is to broaden your understanding of the aging person's mind-set, including the common problem of resistance and how to overcome it.

Chapter 5 tackles the thorny issues of family conflicts about elders. These are common, but few professionals may be looking at these as part of a larger picture—one in which you can be of help. Here I share some examples and show you some ways to work with these problems.

Finally, in Chapter 6, I examine how using tried-and-true conflict resolution techniques can help your aging clients keep their issues from escalating. As an elder mediator myself, I use illustrations to show how you can use mediation, an underutilized resource, to benefit your clients as well as yourself.

Many of my references in this book are to lawyers representing clients. However, I hope that nonlawyers will read this too, with the understanding that much of what applies to lawyers also applies to anyone working with elders. There are universal truths about aging that can work for any professional using this book.

WORKING WITH
AGING
CLIENTS

1

Myths and Stereotypes About Aging

Introduction

What Does It Mean to Be "Old"?

Not all of us understand aging very well, even after it begins to happen to us. Aging or aging well is not part of the curriculum in school, unless one has sought out that field of study. Still, we all have expectations and beliefs about aging, and there are many misconceptions about aging and what is "normal." My effort here is to shed some light on the subject of aging and how individuals are affected by it. We may also learn here to change our expectations and beliefs to allow for greater acceptance of our aging clients—and whether your work is legal, business, finance, or other, you are going to encounter long-lived people as clients. As we increase our understanding of aging in general, we will better understand how to work with our aging clients and those in their lives.

Most of us have a mind-set about aging and what it means. It comes from our social conditioning, our families, and our own beliefs about how aging affects people. Some of these beliefs may be accurate, but some may be based on inaccurate stereotypes, myths, and ideas that can interfere with the professional services we want to offer. This chapter explores some of those common stereotypes and examines how they can interfere with giving each client truly individual treatment and the best possible service.

The Changes of Aging

It is clear that aging is a different experience for each person, just as the process of growing up is unique to each of us. We reach developmental milestones at different times, within a spectrum. A child may learn to walk at nine months, or a year, or even at two years. The range of what is considered "normal" is quite broad. Aging also covers a broad spectrum of change, but it tends to be along a spectrum of physical decline as the body shows the effects of wear and tear. The extent of decline varies a great deal from person to person. Some are vigorous at 95, whereas others are seriously disabled by the changes of aging at 70.

Aging brings with it numerous effects on the brain and nervous system. These changes are normal, but may predispose us to chronic diseases. For example, the brain transmits signals to the rest of the body by way of chemicals called neurotransmitters. With aging, the efficiency of neurotransmitters decreases, causing a slower reaction time to various stimuli.[1] We may see cognitive decline with aging, as discussed in more detail on the section of this chapter dealing with dementia. It is important to distinguish cognitive decline from decline in general intelligence, which is *not* a normal part of aging. In fact, studies indicate that our general intelligence does not diminish as we age unless something interferes with the normal functioning of the brain. Cognitive functioning remains normal and reasoning abilities and judgment are not altered in normal aging.[2]

This fact, in particular, is one that many of us may not expect. It contradicts the stereotypes of aging. We may expect all aging persons to be less capable cognitively, or we may misinterpret slightly slowed processing as diminished cognitive capacity. Though many aging persons do suffer from cognitive impairment, it is helpful for us to recognize that not all individuals experience cognitive decline.

Many of the elders we meet will be cognitively intact and fully capable of participation in decision making. Others will show signs of diminished cognitive function, and we must learn to accommodate this.

---

1. Kathleen McInnis-Ditrich, *Social Work with Elders: A Biopsychosocial Approach to Assessment and Intervention* (Pearson Education, 2005), 32.
2. Patricia Callone et al., *Alzheimer's Disease: 300 Tips for Making Life Easier* (Demos Medical Publishing, 2006), 9.

Society's Attitudes About Aging

Our attitudes about aging form the basis of how we treat elders generally, and particularly how we treat them in our work. If we are to overcome dangerous stereotypes that can diminish our effectiveness, we need to understand what the stereotypes are and how they can affect us as well as others participating in work with aging clients.

American society has always valued productivity. The Puritan work ethic that makes up a fundamental part of our value system does not particularly value those who are no longer "productive" in the sense of working, making money, or raising families. This dismissive attitude often pervades how we treat elders from a financial, medical, social, and even governmental point of view, though this is changing.

We often associate the terms *old* or *elder* with infirmity, loss of competence, and other unfavorable images. This thinking, part of a general cultural outlook on aging, has given rise to the persistent urging to "turn back the clock," "fight aging," "reverse aging," and other anti-aging messages throughout the media.

We do not hear or see a lot of press about celebrating longevity. While it is true that a few exceptional individuals may get media attention for living so long and still contributing to the world, we as a society are far less receptive to images of the old among us than we are to images of younger persons.

The United States is sometimes called a "youth-obsessed culture." Youth pervades commercial messages, entertainment, sports, and print media except when companies are trying to sell to the middle-aged market. The messages all around us seem to tell us that even if you're getting older, it's better to look younger, feel younger, or be younger. Media tend to imprint ideas in our minds. Our stereotypes about aging are influenced by this in ways of which we may not be fully conscious.

The Pervasiveness of Ageism

Advertising pitched to those aged 65 and older is heavily laden with urgings to buy medications, supplements, and assistive devices; it assumes that you must need to function better in your sex life, which you can surely do if you buy their pill.

The unspoken message, repeated endlessly, is that there is something wrong with aging itself. The aging person is portrayed or perceived as less capable, less important, less interesting, or less deserving than a younger, more "productive" person. We characterize these attitudes in our language, as well, with slang that often has negative connotations: "geezer," "old fart," "doddering old fool," "old biddy," "the shuffleboard set," "useless old man," "old codger," "the blue-hair crowd," and even "little old lady" communicate less than a dignified or reverent attitude toward older members of society. The concept that "an old dog can't learn new tricks" is illustrative. It is also untrue.

No one is totally immune from ageist imprinting. To work at developing the deepest respect for the aged among us, we have to expose ourselves to older persons, their achievements, their struggles, their wisdom, and their value. We do this in our daily lives both outside our work and in our direct work with elders in practice or mediation. Developing a respectful attitude and overcoming all the negative messages about aging takes effort. As with other biases and prejudices, we overcome stereotypes regarding aging through intention, self-education, and exposure to the subject of our bias and prejudice. We seek to understand what it must be like to be negatively characterized so pervasively.

As 1970s guru Ram Dass (formerly Richard Alpert) described in his book, *Still Here:*

> As we age, we believe what we're trained to believe about how old people think and live. The Ego gets us to view ourselves as something less than when we were when young, rather than something more. And yet we have the power to age *as we choose*, and to use our changing circumstances to benefit the world and ourselves, if we take the time to know the mind and how it determines the quality of life.[3]

Fear of Aging

It is worthwhile examining our own attitudes about aging to raise awareness of our fears about the aging process. We will be less than effective if we

---

3. Ram Dass, *Still Here* (Berkeley Publishing Group, 2002), 33.

carry a fear of our own aging into our practice as we meet elders. Negative stereotypes can quietly but significantly affect us.

If we have a fear of the loss of control that we think comes with aging, we may project that fear onto anyone we represent. If an elder is being asked to give up an important freedom, we may see ourselves in her shoes and overidentify with her. Acquiring an attitude that is comfortable with aging, even with all the messiness and the duties surrounding it, will allow us to be most effective.

For example, if a conflict breaks out about how a cognitively impaired elder spends his money, and he is perceived by the parties as being vulnerable to manipulation, the issue in the case could be how much control over money the elder should be allowed to retain. If we imagine ourselves in the elder's place and project our own fears about control over money, we might not be able to see the need for those involved to find a way to restrict this particular elder's access to his bank account. We simply need to be aware of how our attitudes affect what we perceive. We can become advocates for something unsafe if we are not aware of our own attitudes.

Our own beliefs require a close, objective look, especially if a client is involved in a case that has elements reflecting experiences we have had in our own lives with persons close to the age of our own parents or grandparents. We do not want our vision of the client before us to be obscured or distorted by our personal negative experiences or fears about growing older.

Stereotypes and the Effect on Elders

The Risk of Not Being Heard

Conflicts, cases, and planning involving elders will be colored by the biases and prejudices of those involved in the matter. Opponents, other players, and parties may be influenced by peers, upbringing, cultural values and beliefs, and society's messages in general about aging, just as we ourselves can be so influenced. Attorneys, family members, caregivers, and associated others can manifest ageist stereotypes in their communications. Positioning as to what is "right" for a particular elder is the effect of these beliefs.

If we are self-aware enough to see past the ageist beliefs that we our-selves may have held, we can see the aging client for who she is, not who we think she might be or should be. We are responsible for observing and limiting the effect of stereotyping and ageism on the elder. The elder may or may not see the negative attitudes toward aging—and may even harbor some of them herself. If the elder is impaired, he may have insufficient men-tal capacity to recognize the effect of such attitudes. If the elder is unable to hear all that is said or to track and process the multiple expressions that fly back and forth as family members or others describe him, he may not have the opportunity to fully voice his ideas and preferences. If the elder is represented, his attorney needs to be that voice and to ensure that it is heard. If the elder is before you alone, your consciousness needs to be tuned in to anything you may be inclined to do that is driven by assumptions about aging people in general. This client may not fit such preconceived ideas.

Even sophisticated professionals working in the field of some aspect of aging or elder-care can possess ageist attitudes. These could directly affect a conflict in a negative way. As an example, I was doing some research for a presentation on the rights of elders to sexual expression in long-term care facilities. I found a number of articles on the subject written by social workers, nurses, and others in the elder-care field. I found various references to elder sexuality in such terms as "the yuck factor" and other negatively characterized terminology. This was from elder-care professionals!

Note that sexuality in a younger person would not likely ever be charac-terized in this way. The negative implication is that if you are older, sexuality and sexual expression are "yucky," but not if you are younger. These words, in professional journal articles, vetted and published for all, reflect exactly what we see all around us. If we are counting on anyone to be free of all negative stereotypes about aging, we are missing the truly ubiquitous nature of ageism.

If we miss the stereotypes, if we let ageism slip by us, the risk to the elder is loss of rights, loss of dignity, and loss of a sense of equality. Even if the elder himself or herself cannot attend every legal proceeding or make every financial or business decision due to physical or cognitive impairment, the elder has a right to a position uncompromised by ageism. The elder's repre-sentative, whether family, attorney, or other, needs to have a fair opportunity to advocate for long-standing beliefs or values of the elder. Simply put, we do not want any elder we represent to be thought of as less valuable, less important, or less worth hearing than anyone else.

The Risk of Social and Emotional Needs Being Overlooked

The risk of the elder's voice being lost or of assumptions about aging taking over the conversation may be very apparent—and quite high—when it comes to the elder's social and emotional needs. In this particular aspect, we as a society seem to deny that our emotions are ageless. As lawyers, I believe we have a particular role in and responsibility for drawing out and upholding the preferences, feelings, values, and beliefs of those we represent. This may well apply to financial planners, business advisors, and others working with elderly clients as well. It is so easy for others to dismiss these things, based on the faulty assumption that they are unimportant or that somehow, with aging, they no longer exist.

For example, the hot-button issue of widowed aging parents' social lives and romantic interests may be an issue in any legal matter involving an elder and her family members. An aging person's need for companionship or love may easily be lost in a dispute about who has the right to decide how Dad is going to spend his money or where he is going to live. Even an incapacitated person who cannot make reasonable money decisions still has emotional needs. The elder's need for enjoyment, company, and other social/emotional aspects of life can often be ignored or drowned out in a fight over other issues concerning safety and care. It is up to the lawyer representing the elder to elicit the elder's preferences and to ensure the elder's right to self-determine, within safe limits, what he or she does about these emotional needs.

If we wish to reduce the risk that elders' social and emotional needs will be overlooked, we need to draw out the elder, or those who care for him or her, to directly address these questions. In my own experience, many elders seem to experience discomfort in talking about feelings, although perhaps not everyone will find this true. I speculate that I have encountered this because the generation we now consider "elders" lived through world wars and the Great Depression, and for much of their lives focused primarily on survival. Talking about their own feelings was just not done. Other serious matters were discussed, but feelings were not emphasized. Perhaps many elders simply never developed a vocabulary for expressing or describing their own emotions. Nevertheless, the social and emotional aspects of an elder's quality of daily life must be a part of any discussion about what should happen to him or her. The issue of where an elder is going to live and be cared for, and by whom, are often the context in which these issues arise.

Raising Our Own Awareness

One can imagine that if the elder's own lawyer has the attitude that any aspect of an elder's rights or any part of an elder's wishes is "yucky," a dispute about these issues might not go so well for the elder. If we find ourselves uncomfortable about any aspect of representing an aging client, we need to ask ourselves the question: "Why does this subject make me feel uncomfortable?" This is an essential part of self-reflection that can enable us to most effectively represent this age cohort without imposing ageist beliefs on them. Should any part of an elder's life or situation bring up uneasy feelings in us that would not be there but for the age of the person before us, it is time to look within for the answer.

We may each have our own blind spots about what it means to age well in our society, with or without the impairments of aging. Do we personally think the elder in question should or should not be placed under a conservatorship/guardianship? Live independently? Give money to some potential heirs and not others? Have the right to be included in discussion about finances when his capacity is impaired? These are issues that require our own understanding while respecting the elder's right to participate in decision making.

For example, you might hear a party or family member say something like "people her age should be in a nursing home." That kind of comment is not unusual, and it is a stereotypical attitude about persons of a certain age. If we ourselves think the same thing, and are not aware of the ageist nature of this belief, we can't possibly be proper legal representatives. It may or may not be true that a particular client has physical and care needs that require a nursing home, but those needs should be determined by examination of the facts and evidence available, rather than on the basis of a predetermined notion of what "should" be.

Overcoming Assumptions About Elders

The Basis of Assumptions About Aging Persons

We are best prepared to work with elders if we are aware of common problems affecting elders, while at the same time making no assumptions that every elder will have these problems. We can't presuppose that a 90-year-old is deaf any more than we can assume that a 70-year-old is mentally sharp. We know that many older persons develop cognitive difficulties as they age, but we cannot assume that every older person does, just because it is common. Nor can we assume that the particular elder we are meeting is like any other elder we have known.

Your own experiences with aging persons can lead to assumptions, even if you do not consider yourself an ageist. One's own negative and positive past contacts with aging persons may give rise to somewhat automatic assumptions about elders in general. We learn from the first older persons we are exposed to in our lives what it means to age or to "be old." Whether we are aware of it later in life or not, we may carry those perceptions and attitudes with us.

Family Experiences with Aging Relatives

If you had a grouchy grandparent, you may unconsciously assume that older people are frequently grouchy. If you had an older relative who was kind and gracious, you may believe that all elders are going to be kind and gracious. If all the older persons you knew in your life had physical difficulties, such as trouble walking or seeing, you may expect that to be true of all the elders you meet going forward in your work. If you had a relative with dementia, you may believe that you know all about the journey of some other person with dementia, though this may be quite untrue. Each person's experience of aging and whatever problems come with it is different. The limited experience of one's own family or neighborhood can narrow our views and keep us stuck in stereotypical thinking.

Because we are products of our own experiences with aging based on others in our lives, we are likely to have incorporated the way others in our lives view aging itself. If your aging relatives had negative experiences of aging, you may have absorbed those attitudes. If you grew up hearing a lot of complaints about aging from someone who was your own elder, it will likely have affected your beliefs. The important thing is to recognize how your experience can influence your work with elders and your effectiveness in problem solving as a lawyer or other professional. It is possible to develop a very empathetic and effective way of working with elders, even if the elders in your own life made you feel that you never wanted to get old.

The Effect of Broadening Our Experience of Older Persons

The only effective way to overcome our own assumptions, whether they are deeply imbedded or not, is to expose ourselves to the world of aging persons in a variety of ways. This can include reading about the aging process, attending events in which the featured speaker is elderly, becoming involved in community activities focused on elders, volunteering with elders, and doing our own research on any part of aging with which we have no experience. As our society ages, and the Baby Boomer generation in particular ages, the opportunities to learn more about elders and aging increase. Exposure to different kinds of aging persons enables us to work more effectively with this population because we can recognize and discard our assumptions as we find people who contradict them.

Examining Our Feelings About Our Own Aging

In addition to broadening our view of elders in general, it is useful to examine how we feel about our own aging. We can take the time to reflect upon what relationships with aging persons have been like in our families and social groups. We can check in with our own attitudes by first raising our awareness of them. If anything about aging, from the way it changes your bodies to the way it can cause your health to decline, is something that makes you cringe or turn away, it's time to examine why and to learn within yourself how this reaction can be changed. We need to value the process and personal impact of aging if we are to be effective in working with aging individuals. We need to be very cautious about reacting to aging with fear, as so many people in our society do.

The broadening of our experience with elders in general has the positive effect of helping us overcome stereotypes, as well as helping us to accept and understand our own aging process. With an accepting attitude about our own aging, we are freer to encourage and suggest positive ways for our clients and their families to work out age-related issues and conflicts. We can see our aging clients in the same way we would see anyone else, but with a unique set of issues. Financial issues might focus more on making money last for years longer than expected or paying for long-term care. This kind of problem may not arise until a client is of advanced age. For example, legally, a client may lose her ability to be the trustee of the family trust; we need to appreciate that special circumstance connected to disabilities that often—but not always—accompany aging. Generally, we must be "tuned in" to what is likely to happen with our aging clients but not assume that anything we anticipate will always affect every aging client.

Medical Stereotyping of Elders

Stereotyping of elders is not limited to laypersons, those with less education, or those who do not work with elders. As a part of our society, medical professionals may fall victim to the same biased mind-set about aging as anyone else. Outside the specialized area of geriatric medicine, doctors may dismiss complaints from elders with "you're just getting old." Adult children may not perceive the dangers of their aging parents' social isolation, depression, loss of a sense of purpose, and need for many kinds of assistance because physicians are not helpful or even knowledgeable about these issues. If the doctor isn't concerned about an elder's complaints, the family or others in the elder's life may not be either.

My mother-in-law, age 92 at the time I write this, became very upset with a doctor she saw for a particular complaint. Rather than listening respectfully and working with her on the problem, he said, "What do you expect? You're 92." She was more than a little annoyed by his response and never went back. Unfortunately, this doctor's attitude is not unusual.

The concerns of elders can be affected by dismissive attitudes toward them from health-care professionals. These attitudes may be reflected by various caregivers and family who are involved in the daily lives of elders. Conflicts can arise over an elder's condition, care, independence, and needs. Elders themselves may feel less valued because they do not receive the same attention from a physician or other health-care provider that a younger person might. What is best for an elder and what is wrong or not wrong with the elder is a frequent source of conflict. Medical stereotyping can both create and exacerbate conflicts with and about elders.

Illustration: Richard's Case

Richard, an 85-year-old, saw his doctor because he had been losing weight. He wanted to continue to live in his own home and was willing to let others help him, but he was struggling. His family was complaining that he shouldn't live by himself anymore. His doctor saw Richard for about 20 minutes, did some superficial testing, and concluded that Richard should go to a senior living community, which he pushed Richard to do. No time was taken to explore what Richard wanted, which was to remain in his own home. No effort was made to explore the options available other than giving up his home. The family agreed with what the doctor told them and Richard's preferences were ignored.

"The doctor said" became a very aggravating source of conflict in the family, despite the fact that the doctor in a busy clinic was not likely to have taken the time to consider Richard's need to make up his own mind about possibly giving up his home. We concluded that Richard's wishes had been disregarded and dismissed because of his age and the assumption that he could not manage at home, even if a good support system were put in place. No opportunity to try out what the elder wanted was going to be allowed. Lawyers for the family and for Richard were hired. The ugly battle that ensued could have been avoided.

This illustration typifies how quickly some medical professionals dismiss the voice of the elder in favor of their own, preconceived notions of what it means to be old. Typically, the physician's opinion, whether or not truly informed or respectful of the elder, carries a lot of weight with those in the elder's life. Unfortunately, many physicians are not specifically educated to work with elders, and stereotypes about aging can affect their recommendations and interactions with aging persons in ways that are far from ideal—and may even be unwittingly harmful.

In the preceding example, the family had repeatedly argued with Richard that he needed to go to a care facility. He had considered doing so, but wasn't quite ready to take that step yet. The family pitted themselves against him, basing their arguments in part on the doctor's rather superficial examination, which did not go far enough to explore the reasons *why* Richard had been losing weight. Richard's attorney had a more comprehensive examination of his mental status done by a mental health professional in order to obtain a better picture of Richard's ability to care for himself. The examining psychologist found Richard competent to make his own decisions. He needed some help at home with meal preparation, but was competent to decide when it was time to give up his home and move to a care facility. When he got the help at home that he needed, he gained weight and managed for a time until he made his own decision to move.

This example also illustrates how the "too old to live by himself anymore" stereotype was adopted, first by the treating medical doctor and next by the family members, who ignored their father's wishes and took steps to force him to move. They failed, but this bitter family struggle and the legal expenses incurred in Richard's stand for his right to independence could have been avoided.

On the opposite side of the picture is the physician who may have known the elder for many years and is unwilling to state that he or she is no longer competent to make certain decisions, such as financial decisions. It is my experience that most medical doctors do not take the time—nor can they take the time in a routine office visit—to assess an elder's competence regarding decision making. As discussed in later chapters, mental health professionals are best suited to do testing that provides reliable, objective data with which to measure competence for specific tasks. It is risky for anyone, including the elder, to rely exclusively on the long-time primary care doctor, internist, or cardiologist to make such a decision about competence. Some physicians will decline to say anything one way or the other. Others may opine that the elder "seems fine" after a short visit, adding nothing to the effort by others to determine the elder's true capacity for making decisions. Some may have their own stereotypical beliefs about their patients, such as that unless they complain of being impaired, they should be allowed to remain independent in all things. Either way, whether dismissing the elder's right to be independent too quickly or glossing over concerns raised by others regarding the elder, the physician may or may not help with ageist perspectives that lead to disputes.

Addressing Medical Stereotyping

When we are faced with a conflict such as described in these examples, in which the medical assessment of an elder is an issue, it may be helpful to suggest getting a second opinion from a physician who specializes in working with elders. When a dispute exists, it is possible that medical stereotyping can worsen the conflict or be inadequate to answer the questions that lie at the heart of the conflict. The elder's right to self-determination may necessitate obtaining additional information so that you have better information to help keep your client safe.

You are likely to be in the position of trusted professional with your older clients and their families. If you sense, from what your client tells you about something that affects your work, that a physician has a dismissive attitude, take the initiative to suggest getting a second opinion from a physician who specializes in working with elders. Although geriatricians are sometimes hard to find, that would be a first choice for getting another opinion. The geriatrician's special training in the medical issues of aging patients will give the client a better chance at solving whatever medical problem is at hand, or at least addressing it fairly. Your suggestions and recommendations matter to your clients.

Here is another example of how a physician, though well-meaning, can harm an elder.

Illustration: Jeanine's Case

Jeanine, age 85, has been in conflict with her daughters for some time. She refuses to sign any legal documents, such as a power of attorney allowing them to help her manage her finances or any other aspect of her life. She has fallen repeatedly, has memory loss problems, and forgets to turn off the stove and the faucet. She fails to take prescribed medications. Her daughter, Janet, has been urging her to go to the doctor, and in fact finally got Jeanine to go by personally driving her to the doctor's office. Jeanine hadn't seen the doctor for nearly a year, despite Janet's urgings.

Prior to the visit, Janet wrote a letter to the doctor, spelling out the specifics of why she was worried about her mother, describing the dangers at home, and asking for his help in talking to Jeanine about signing a release of information so Janet could talk directly to the doctor about her mother. Instead, the doctor advised Jeanine not to sign anything! Now Janet must seek a new doctor who takes Jeanine's Medicare plan and set up an appointment, all with resistance from Jeanine. Seeing that unhelpful doctor made a bad situation worse and made Janine even less safe. The doctor had a careless attitude toward Jeanine and may not have recognized the obvious signs of dementia pointed out in Janet's letter.

A fair-minded doctor would have taken the family member's report seriously and would have spent some time with the elder going over the problems raised in the letter. In addition, the doctor could have ordered some neuropsychological testing to determine whether there was indeed cognitive impairment. Unfortunately, this doctor's action exacerbated the dispute between the elder and her daughters. The situation was headed toward guardianship, as there was physical danger to Jeanine from the stove and water left on.

Conclusion

Stereotypes about aging are everywhere. It is very likely that we will encounter unfair attitudes and beliefs about aging in our work. We can overcome the negative effects of our society's ageist attitudes by first becoming conscious of our own attitudes, reflecting on them, and raising our personal awareness of how these beliefs can interfere with a fair process for elders. Our unique responsibility is to aim for fairness, first from ourselves, as the legal representatives or other professionals, and then from all others involved in the conflicts we encounter concerning elders. If there is an issue in which you are not directly involved, but you know what might make a difference for the client, speak up. Serving our clients as best we can is always our business. Whether others listen to our suggestions is up to them, but we serve best if we offer what guidance we can.

2

Challenges in Working with Elders

Introduction

Work with aging clients involves special challenges, both those created by the aging persons themselves and those arising from our own attitudes. We need to be conscious of what it means to have impairments and to need accommodation. This chapter addresses aging and how elderly clients differ from other clients. We look here at how an open attitude and consciousness of an aging client's possible difficulties can foster the elder's maximum participation in your professional-client interactions. We consider what accommodations aging clients might need and how to anticipate those needs. We look at elders' quality-of-life issues and our consciousness of how to communicate respect. Representing and advocating for elders requires awareness of how to adapt to a person who may not be able to participate in attorney-client interactions as easily as a younger person can.

Background

Since volunteering in a nursing home beginning at age 14, I have always found it a privilege to work with aging persons. Over the years of meeting so many elders as a nurse and visiting them in their homes, I developed a perspective of appreciating the wide range of what to expect and how different one person of a particular age could be in both physical condition and mental state from another person of the same age. Not everyone has the advantage of such a perspective in the practice of law, financial advising, or business. We may find ourselves working with clients and being surprised by or unprepared for their age-related difficulties. We may forget that age can affect everything we do with and for elderly clients, from how we present information to them to how to earn their respect, trust, and appreciation. Learning about aging clients as we represent or work with them, rather from another source, is challenging.

In this chapter I share some of my experiences and views of working with elders, particularly those who have disabilities and impairments. My intention is to flatten your learning curve and permit your own aging clients to feel respected right away. If one understands what to watch for, communication and interaction will be easier for the professional.

The vulnerability caused by aging in the elders we meet is often accompanied by the beauty of their wisdom, rich life experience, and strength. Even difficult persons may have depth in their life stories, which colors their perceptions of how they are treated, what they appreciate, and what they are willing to do. Finding that depth and helping them to appreciate their own needs is part of what makes representing or working with elders a satisfying experience. You need not have extensive background in working with elders to develop the sensitivity necessary to be effective. It is helpful, however, to familiarize yourself with general aspects of aging and how it may influence what you say and do for the client. Raising our consciousness of any special needs will assist us in demonstrating to our clients that we have what it takes to do the job they need done.

My own grandmother had an extensive influence on me and my perspective on aging. She handled aging well and created an impression that aging could be a positive time in life. I learned informally at her knee some of the things that current research has shown us about positive aspects of aging. My positive experience with an aging person led me to my lifelong interest in elders. Perhaps a positive influence in your own life has led you to seek information about working with aging persons. Perhaps you are just seeing more of them in your practice or your files because our general population is aging, and you realize that we all need to be ready to represent and help more older clients. Whatever your background or area of professional practice, all life experience can assist you in understanding aging and doing the best job with and for clients of advanced age. You can add awareness and consciousness of aging itself to your personal experiences with family members who are older, as well as with aging clients. My hope is that your deepened awareness will permit you to anticipate problems and prevent interactions with aging people in your practice from becoming unnecessarily difficult. With education and awareness, we develop successful strategies.

Negative Aspects of Working with Aging Clients

Although my own experience with a grandparent was positive, years of being a visiting (home health) nurse also brought me face-to-face with the difficult and negative impacts of aging. The struggle to keep elders safe as they declined was apparent. I observed the complexities of multiple medical conditions coexisting at the same time in one body. I saw how costly it was for those around them to take care of these elders as health declined. Some outlived their modest pensions and had to face poverty, something they had never thought could happen. Or they had to spend retirement savings on caregivers and were terrified that they would have nothing left if they kept on living—and yet they did live on and on. I noticed how overwhelmed and frustrated their caregivers could get. I saw how frustrated the seniors got with being unable to do things they had always done independently. Most people hated becoming dependent, and some stayed angry about it. Later, as I entered the field of elder mediation, I began to see how the effort to protect aging persons, the vulnerability of aging, and the financial cost of caring for elders created fear, confusion, and conflict for both the elders and those caring for them.

These difficulties may be hidden from the view of most professionals, including lawyers and other service providers, because we generally see clients in our offices. If we go to the person's home, we are there to attend to a specific task. We leave when that task is completed and usually do not get exposed to their more complex personal business. We may not be aware of their medical diagnoses, their multiple medications, or their fears about getting older and losing control over their lives. We may believe that their personal problems are none of our business. However, I have observed that what is going on in clients' personal lives almost invariably affects their participation in any case or business matter. It is helpful to consider the reasons why a client is difficult. Showing concern for clients' personal, "nonbusiness" problems is one way you can earn their trust. When you demonstrate respect and concern, they will feel it. Everyone needs to be understood, especially those who have impairments, communication difficulties, or other limitations that most younger persons do not experience.

Everything from physical pain to fear about losing control, to frustration with being incapacitated in any way, to worries about finances and other considerations can color older clients' interactions with the professionals who work with them. While these same worries can affect any client, in an older person they may occur together, piling up and becoming more overwhelming than for a younger person who possibly has more physical and financial resources, and may have more ability to recover from losses. Typically, a younger client is less dependent on others for help in daily life than the person of advanced years. Of course, elders vary in all of these things, and it is difficult to generalize; one cannot just assume that any particular elder has any or all of these problems. However, older people are at greater risk for physical and mental decline simply because of aging itself, so it falls to the professional to investigate each client's situation. Physical issues, in particular, may create continuous stress and affect the older client's emotions, behavior, and willingness to engage in stressful decision making with a lawyer, financial advisor, accountant, or other professional. Mental decline can deprive an elder of the very ability we need our clients to have when working with us on a legal or business matter of any kind. These problems cannot be ignored.

During my 27 years of litigation practice, I encountered a steady stream of aging clients, as I am located in a county with a large aging population. I was constantly reminded of the need to make accommodations for these seniors, whether it was within my own office, from opposing counsel, or from those connected to any case involving an elder. Sometimes clients were difficult due to reasons that had nothing to do with the case. Some of the problems I encountered included resistance to change, slowness in processing information, and the inability to participate in proceedings for average time periods.

Older clients can be irritable, forgetful, and physically unable to sit for long periods. They might have hearing or visual impairments. They might express impatience with us, with the legal proceeding, with other lawyers, or with the requirements of the law we are obligated to follow. Some are depressed for various reasons, such as loss of a spouse or loss of physical capacity. The depressed clients often had trouble making decisions or staying focused on the matter at hand. Some seemed easily confused, particularly by complex legal issues. This was not necessarily due to any form of brain disease (such as dementia, which we discuss in greater detail in a subsequent chapter); rather, it was due to a reduced ability to process information at the same rate as a younger person.

All of these issues may require that we change the way we do things for an aging client. We may need to take more time with them; educate opposing counsel, our office colleagues, and others involved in our clients' need for accommodation; and lead the way in demonstrating patience and understanding of what our client needs to be properly represented and respectfully treated. If there is a single quality I can suggest that the law-yer or other professional work on in dealing with aging clients, it is simply *patience*. This couples well with the ability to listen. Take your time. Do not schedule a "quick appointment." Allow for a slower processing time for information you wish to provide. Reassure the client that you will be with the conversation for as long as she needs you to be.

Family Dynamics in Working with Elders

Because many persons of advanced age need physical assistance, they often are accompanied by a family member when interacting with a lawyer or business professional—and not just estate-planning lawyers. For example, if an elder needs help walking, the family member whose arm is supporting him will be with the client when you meet. Thus, relationships with adult children and spouses come into play. Some of these are dysfunctional and add another layer of difficulty to our communication with aging clients.

Elders and family members who all maintain a positive outlook may be very helpful to you in working with or representing the aging client. However, some family members create conflict and can interfere with the decisions the older client must make in any business matter, legal or otherwise. Working with elders can raise very complex problems that go beyond legal questions. Family dynamics can interfere with your efforts to do the right thing for the aging client. A domineering spouse of a frail elder, or an officious adult child, may try to control what the aging person does. The elder may be or feel vulnerable and may be pressured into choices he does not really prefer.

Looking out for the best interests of an aging client may require that we insist on speaking to the client outside the presence of the family member even when the law does not specifically require this. The aging client's voice can easily be drowned out by an overbearing family member who believes that he or she knows what's best for the aging loved one and may also assume that he or she knows what the elder wants. Overbearing family or others can influence you, too. Do not take what they tell you at face value. Ask your client to confirm it, but at the same time understand that trying to find the truth may take more than one conversation. Your aging client may or may not have subtle memory-loss issues that are not apparent in a single conversation.

Helpful Attitudes You Can Adopt

An open mind about aging clients can be formed from your own history or from more recent experience. Some helpful attitudes toward aging persons are bolstered by current literature. Research assists us to learn about positive aging and to see that aging persons are capable of problem solving, contrary to those stereotypes we have mentioned. Those who are cognitively intact can often do as well as or even better than a younger person. For example, in his book *The Mature Mind*, psychiatrist Gene Cohen, MD, PhD, says, "It turns out that not only can old dogs learn well, they are actually better at many types of intellectual tasks than younger dogs."[1]

Cohen has studied and written about the uplifting perspective that aging is a time of expansion, rather than simply a physical decline. Dr. Cohen and those who share his views see aging as a time of recognizing potential beyond the problems associated with aging. It can be a time of positive change, growth, and increased engagement in life. This work helps us understand that the elders we represent can help us. If we communicate effectively with them, assuming that they are capable of full participation in their cases and other matters, their engagement in problem solving can facilitate all of

---

1. Gene D. Cohen, *The Mature Mind: The Positive Power of the Aging Brain* (Basic Books 2005), xv.

the decision making that must be done. This is one positive and stereotype-busting reality we can embrace.

Despite the perception that elders are invariably "set in their ways," one can find surprising flexibility in competent elders. Even with the cognitive impairments that affect so many persons living to advanced age, there are periods of lucidity, cooperation, and willingness that may allow us to do our work with elders effectively. As we encounter persons with cognitive impairment in our work, we learn to focus on what *ability* the elder still has, rather than what he or she has lost. As one of my clients put it when speaking about her mother with early dementia, "She may have dementia, but she still has a mind of her own."

Creativity and creative thinking can blossom at any age. Involving elders in the decisions needed to complete their legal and business matters must always be considered, even when their abilities are not all still completely intact. This is not only because self-determination is a basic tenet of what we want to honor in our clients, but also because we do not want to short-change the problem-solving process by overlooking an elder's ability to devise solutions. Our own attitude of consideration of elders' creative thinking can help. We need to invite them into the process of working through a legal case, a financial decision, or any other matter when this is possible and to the greatest extent possible. Even when impairments exist, we serve aging clients best by respecting the reality of any impairment while offering the client the chance to provide his or her input. Our own judgment as to the value of that input is essential, of course, but we do not want to cut off any client's chance to think through problems with us, as we could thereby miss something unique from that client.

The Professional's Role: Remembering Quality of Life for Elders

An often-overlooked aspect of Working with Aging Clients and those who care for them and about them is the question of what makes life enjoyable as people age. Healthy aging includes expanding one's social network, finding meaningful activity, and having fun. Those involved with aging family members or friends may spend all their energy concentrating on the legal case at hand, the investment decisions, the business, safety, caregiving, control of assets, and other issues, to the exclusion of the fundamental need of elders to enjoy their lives. The lawyer representing the aging client can be the one to remind family members to look at the overall picture of how a case, a trust, a successor trustee, a settlement, a real estate matter, or other matter will affect the aging person's life once the legal business is completed. This is not exactly what the law demands of us. Rather, it is what being a compassionate representative demands of us. Lawyers can serve as counselors in reminding family members to remain aware of the elder's needs even after the legal matter reaches its conclusion.

Other professionals handling finances, or business dealings of any kind, can take on a similar role. For those who have known the client well over many years, this is especially appropriate: to articulate the elder's long-standing values and beliefs, patterns, and investment philosophy. You have a working knowledge based on your experience with the client and you are in a good position to advocate for your client's quality of life. Please speak up. Your client's personal life can become your business if you care to allow this. If your client does not want you to offer your opinions and suggestions, accept that. But I would much prefer any professional in an elder's life to take an active role in ensuring the best for that client, rather than seeing the professional stand idly by when anyone else overlooks obvious needs or takes advantage of an elder. The worst that may happen is that someone tells you not to stick your nose in that part of your client's business. So what? There is no harm in trying to do the right thing. Your long-standing relationship with an aging client you know well can give you a valuable perspective on many things.

What Elders Need

Physical limitations such as hearing loss, vision impairment, and difficulty with mobility do not take away a person's need to have fun. The quality of an elder's life will be dictated, in part, by what enjoyable activities he or she can participate in and choose for the sake of the pleasure they bring.

Despite illnesses or limitations, during this time of life people are still driven by powerful forces, such as the desires for love, companionship, self-determination, control, and giving back. In working with them, and in particular when interacting with their family members, it is helpful to introduce these quality-of-life questions. They can be strong motivators of an elder's position in any legal proceeding or other matter when a decision is required, though they may be unspoken.

Recognizing What Is Different About Elders

We don't want to embrace society's stereotypes about aging, but at the same time we need to accept that aging persons are at much higher risk for physical, mental, and emotional decline than are most younger persons. Aging changes the body, and it can also change cognition. The older a person gets, the more he or she is at risk for age-related diseases and impairments.

The law provides special protections for those deemed "elders," defined by the government as those over the age of 65. Medicare and Social Security are available to Americans aged 65 and over. The assumption built into these laws is that elders are in need of such special protections and benefits. The intent of our legislatures in devising such elder-specific laws and provisions is to protect elders from the vulnerabilities associated with aging.

Although we cannot assume that every elder is vulnerable due to aging, we can expect that some elders we meet will be more vulnerable than others. Their age-related declines in health and capacity expose them to various risks, including abuse and neglect. Vulnerable elders are at a disadvantage due to loss of independence and the need to receive care or help with daily activities from others. Although some elders may remain independent until the end of their lives, we can expect to see elderly clients with significant physical and mental capacity issues.

Watch for Vulnerabilities

Our responsibility in working with elders is to watch for vulnerabilities even if the elder does not express them. If an aging client comes to us with a legal matter, we need to consider the person's age and what things we might need to do to give adequate representation. If your long-standing client asks for your guidance, you have an enhanced responsibility. If the client who needs your help is 95 years old, you will have to seek information you might not necessarily consider requesting from a client who is 45. Our responsibility to persons of advanced age includes ensuring that any elder who may have difficulty expressing himself has a voice; it also requires that we see the issues affecting the elder in the context of a potential need for protections contemplated by law. You do not have to be a lawyer to embrace this responsibility. It is an ethical consideration: the "right thing" to do.

Various questions might come up in interviewing any aging client.

1. Is there any difficulty in communicating with this client, such as hearing or understanding?
2. Can the person get to my office, manage a certain walking distance, or go up stairs if there is no elevator?
3. Does the client show any evidence of a memory problem or difficulty in keeping track of the conversation?
4. Is anyone accompanying the client pushing him to do things?

If you are already aware of possible problems, and are alert about looking for them, you are more likely to see them and be able to adjust for them. Generally, we may have to rely on information from more than one source to determine whether a client of advanced years is able to fully manage interacting with us or if she might need some help. Likewise, we may have to obtain additional information pertaining to the facts or legal question at hand from someone other than the elder. It is not safe to assume that every elder is totally independent, totally capable of making safe decisions, and not in need of help from anyone else when you get involved in her matter. We would probably all like to be completely independent and competent forever, as would our clients, but age can and does take its toll. We simply need to honor that truth as it applies to each individual client.

The Risk of Reliance on Elders' Self-Reported Information

When we first encounter an elder in a telephone call or meeting, we ask questions to obtain information about the legal or business matter and why they have contacted us. With aging clients, we need to keep in the back of our minds the possibility that we will also have to seek information about them or their matter from someone other than the elder. Self-reported information from elders, particularly about their abilities when they suffer from dementia, can be unreliable. Judgment, recall of events, and level of insight into their capabilities can be impaired and can affect self-reported information.

Even an elder who seems perfectly competent while talking with you on the phone could have impairments that would affect your ability to effectively represent them or do work for them. It is difficult to be sure of an elder's capacity to participate in a case from a single telephone call or isolated encounter. It is generally helpful to ask the client some basic questions about her ability to manage things at home and whether she has help there. If the aging client tells you she has "a few problems remembering" or that she got lost coming to your office, take these as some early-warning signs that the elder could have impairments and may need help with the legal or business matter. Some elders overestimate their abilities, both physical and regarding mental capacity.

I was reminded of this when attending a bar association annual function recently. A venerable and respected lawyer in our community attended. I saw him leaving at the end of the event using his walker. I spoke with his daughter, an elder herself, and said hello to her father. "He's doing pretty well for 98," she said. She mentioned that she helps him with his shopping now, but he still plans and cooks all his meals. I imagine that it would be a challenge to figure out whether this 98-year-old lawyer had any cognitive impairment. He is very independent and probably still does some legal work. He is frail, though, and that is a warning sign that would simply make me want to ask more than the usual questions if I had to do some work for him. I would not make any snap judgments about whether or not he was competent merely based on saying "hello" and hearing from his daughter that he could still do the cooking at home.

Confidentiality

The legal requirement of confidentiality becomes an issue immediately when working with an elder who seems to have some impairments of the abilities needed to participate in a legal matter. This applies to anyone managing finances for an aging client as well. Asking about trusted family members who could help or who are already involved with the elder is essential. A written waiver of confidentiality can be obtained from the client. The main point here is that you do not want to assume that an elder is perfectly capable of making decisions in a case without help when you have doubts from the beginning. Awareness of what to look for is crucial to a lawyer's ability to proceed safely with an aging client. In contrast, some elders remain fully mentally capable until the end of life, and you will not have any reason to doubt their capacity. The balance needed in the lawyer's assessment is to understand that capability to participate and make decisions in a legal matter may be there and it may not. If it is not, the aging client will need help from a trusted other, and it is your responsibility to get that help for the client.

Other professionals in an elder's life also have the responsibility of confidentiality. I encourage you to obtain your client's permission early on in your dealings with him, so that you can call upon another trusted person he has chosen to help him should the need arise. You need to get your client's permission to use your judgment about contacting someone she has appointed for this purpose, even if the legal requirements for transition of power from your client to a successor trustee or agent have not been formally fulfilled. Meeting those legal requirements, which normally involves seeing one or two doctors and getting the requisite certifications, can take time, and time can expose a client to dangerous exploitation.

The point here is the relationship between you and your client and the trust he or she has in your judgment. A waiver of confidentiality should be sought before doubts about a client's competency arise, so that it is in place when needed. If you have your client's permission to contact a third party, the appointed successor trustee, or agent on a durable power of attorney or other document, do not hesitate to use it. However, be particularly cautious if the appointed person does not appear to you to be trustworthy. Discussion of problems in this regard, focused on possible elder abuse, appears in later chapters.

Physical Limitations

It is not unusual for a lawyer to encounter a client who has physical limitations, particularly in personal injury cases or disability matters. A client with disabilities can present in any matter. What is different about working with elders is the frequency with which our clients have physical impairments. For other professionals, your aging clients may develop limitations over time, as you work with them sometimes for decades.

Most of us experience physical changes ourselves as we pass age 40, such as needing reading glasses, or not being as physically fit as we were at a younger age. With aging persons, we more often see hearing loss, vision impairment of some type, and mobility problems than in younger people. Stamina may be lessened. Attention span can also be decreased. These bring up the need for accommodation, which is discussed later in this section.

It can be very difficult for an unimpaired person to appreciate the experience of having the physical impairments that many elders must live with. I was reminded of this when I was asked to consult on a project involving product development for elders and caregivers.

Creating Impairments to Mimic Real Life

The product development company conducted a "think tank," and invited people from a broad variety of walks of life to offer ideas for inventing new products. To prepare all the participants, the company wanted each of us to know what it is like to be in the population their products serve: elders. In other words, they wanted us to experience the equivalent of impairments that older persons often have to deal with every day.

We each received a box with items we were asked to put on or try. We were to do specific chores with the items on. We then made notes of our reaction to the effort and whether we were able to carry out the assigned chores. The box contained a thick pair of scratched and blurry goggles, to simulate visual impairment; we could not read or watch TV with them on. There were earplugs, so that we could experience what it's like to have hearing loss. There were adult incontinence products (diapers), which we wore to see what they felt like (hot and uncomfortable!). There were thick garden gloves, so that we could experience trying to do something like cooking while being unable to grasp well, simulating what it is like to have arthritis or diminished sensation in the hands. There were rocks to put in our shoes, so we could feel what it is like to walk with a mobility impairment.

The experience of using these devices was frustrating, to say the least. To not be able to see or hear well was irritating. I wanted to take off the goggles and earplugs and throw them at the wall. I wanted to rip away all the things that limited my senses and abilities. Of course the elders with whom we work can't get rid of these impairments, no matter how frustrated they may be. This experiment was a reminder that sitting, standing, getting around, hearing what is going on, and seeing or reading everything before them may not be as easy for elders as it is for younger persons. This physical experience was an excellent lesson and reminder of the need to accommodate our aging clients' disabilities.

Accommodating the Elder's Stamina Limitations

Interviewing your aging client by phone may not tell you as much as meeting him face-to-face will tell you. Observe your client or potential client. Note how he sits in the chair. Is he squirming uncomfortably? Does he need to get up after a short time? Most of us as professionals are quite used to sitting at our desks all day long. We don't think about it much unless we ourselves have physical limitations, such as back pain or arthritis. We may attend depositions that go on for hours. We may sit in conferences and meetings that drag on and on. Your aging client is far less likely to be able to do this than the average lawyer or advisor who sits in a chair all day. Being aware of this can influence how long you meet with an elder and how long you allow for any proceeding involving him that you arrange.

How do you know whether your client needs to be accommodated for stamina? *Ask.* "How long are you able to sit without getting uncomfortable or tired?" You might also ask, "If we have to go to a hearing and it takes a few hours, do you think you could sit there that long?" Find out your client's best time of day. Many elders are better in the morning but become fatigued later in the day; others take a while to "get going" and are more alert in the afternoon. Individuals vary. It is respectful to find out what your client's habits are and to work at arranging any proceeding according to her needs. Keep the time for whatever you plan shorter than you would with a younger person.

In one example of this, an elderly man who had both physical disabilities and difficulty tracking a conversation did participate in a conference involving several parties. By arrangement with his attorney, a caregiver brought the elder to the proceeding in his wheelchair. His attorney invited him to speak and describe his wishes at the appropriate time. The elder said a few words, stayed about an hour, and then was excused with the caregiver. All present were able to accommodate his needs while still permitting his voice to be heard. He was not pushed beyond his stamina limits.

Mental Capacity Limitations

A frequent issue in working with elders is the question of whether the elder's mental capacity is impaired, and if so to what extent. Mental impairment may be the cause of the legal issue that gives rise to the need for representation in the first place. It may also be an issue of whether the elder can participate in important decision making. This is a difficult area for attorneys and others because there is no easy or sure way to make determinations or even diagnoses of declining mental capacity.

Elders present a unique set of problems in the area of determining mental capacity. We do not know enough scientifically about how to fully assess capacity in general. We have particular difficulty in determining financial decision-making capacity. Metrics are being developed, but the use of metrics is not an everyday occurrence in the lives of elders. Capacity for anyone is affected by changes in the brain, such as with dementia or after a stroke, but there is neither a single nor a definitive way to get an absolute answer as to whether an impaired person has or does not have capacity for a particular task or decision.

We cannot see into the functions of the elder's brain and its billions of connections while it is working, making it almost impossible to reach any easy or certain conclusions about the exact extent of any impairment or damage. We rely on what we can see instead: how an elder behaves, how an elder relates to others, what decisions he or she makes, how the elder appears to be managing the ordinary tasks of everyday life, and how life-long patterns appear to be changing, whether suddenly or over time.

Legal Considerations of Mental Capacity

The starting point in the law is a presumption that adults possess the capacity to undertake any legal task they choose or make any decision they want to make, unless they have been adjudicated incompetent (incapacitated) to perform the task. Such an adjudication takes place in the context of guardianship or conservatorship, or when a party challenging the elder's capacity puts forward sufficient evidence of incapacity in a legal proceeding to meet a requisite burden of proof. Across jurisdictions, *legal capacity* has multiple definitions, set out in either state statutory and/or case law.[2]

Capacity is also a broad term that may include many kinds of decision-making capability. Financial capacity is a specific issue that frequently arises with elders; it often puzzles those who are trying to pin down whether a person's ability is fully intact, partially intact, or diminished enough that we need to remove her choice to make financial decisions.

Vague definitions of financial capacity in the law exemplify how difficult this particular ability is to measure. Financial capacity represents a broad continuum of activities and specific skills. A person may be competent to undertake some of the financial activities of his life, but not others.[3]

Some lawyers may be especially misguided about this because of the fairly loose standard the law applies when judging whether a person has the capacity to make a will or trust. Most doubt about this is resolved in favor of the client who wishes to make the will, as the courts do not require that a person understand all the nuances of his financial status nor that he even be able to balance his checkbook. A person can still make a will or trust as long as he has a generally good idea of what he owns and to whom he wants to give it after his death. In contrast, financial capacity is another matter. It is a very complex issue, which I address later in this chapter.

2. ABA Commission on Law & Aging & American Psychological Association, *Assessment of Older Adults with Diminished Capacity: A Handbook for Psychologists* (2005), 16.
3. Daniel C. Marson, et al., Assessing Financial Capacity in Patients with Alzheimer Disease: A Conceptual Model and Prototype Instrument, *Archives of Neurology*, vol. 57, p. 878 (June 2000).

Neuropsychological Testing for Capacity

Neuropsychological testing (using groups of related tests) can provide useful information to take the question of capacity outside the realm of speculation. Some nominally objective way to measure brain function is far better than collecting the conflicting opinions of family, interested persons, and the elders themselves, none of whom may be able to judge capacity fairly or reliably.

Testing can provide data about which parts of a person's cognitive function do or do not compare normally with the function of persons of similar age and education. Psychologists and neuropsychologists are the only individuals licensed to administer such tests. A few test instruments help delineate whether a person is safe in handling investments or balancing the checkbook. Administering these tests can help us learn how an individual stacks up in test performance compared with others of the same age and educational level. However, a person can test in the normal range on some metrics and still be unsafe in making decisions of various kinds, especially complex contractual or financial decisions.

The question of whether an aging client is impaired weighs heavily on any attorney who wants to represent an aging client but has concerns about that client's ability to participate in a legal matter. Such matters invariably involve making decisions, often financial decisions with significant consequences. It also weighs particularly heavily on those who manage finances for elders and who must get a client's permission to proceed with a financial transaction.

The "Gray Zone"

Physicians, psychologists, courts, and lawyers alike struggle with the nebulous dimensions of determining financial and other kinds of capacity. Capacity can change from one day to the next, just as a person's mood or behavior can. Unlike determining testamentary capacity (the ability to make a will), a determination that an elder is fully capable of independently making safe financial decisions may require not only the input of experts, but also input from those who observe the elder on a daily basis.

In a state I call "the gray zone," the elder is both partly capable and partly lacking in good judgment. Drawing the line and deciding about this issue when the answer is neither black nor white must be a judgment call by those best able to make that call. The best a lawyer faced with this question can do is to thoroughly interview the client with specific items in mind; to collect information from sources other than the client when possible; and, if doubts remain, to request testing to gather more information.

For others, particularly financial professionals, your organization or institution should have a policy in place to guide you when there is doubt about an aging person's financial capacity. At the minimum, you should know the warning signs or "red flags" that would suggest to you that a client may have memory loss or dementia. You will need to have a standardized way of responding when these red flags are present. This requires education and training so that you do not unwittingly engage your client in decisions she is not fully capable of understanding. In organizations that involve management of an elder's finances, protecting the elder from unnecessary risk is paramount, especially when cognitive impairment could make it impossible for the aging client to understand or appreciate the risk.

It is imperative for any ethical professional to be on the alert for cognitively impaired elders who may be misunderstood by your colleagues. If, after reading this book and using other resources to increase your awareness, you have a better understanding of financial capacity than the next person, *please share it*. I have seen too many lawyers who lack sufficient knowledge of financial capacity be naively drawn into doing what a client wants when the client is not fully capable of making a safe financial decision. These lawyers usually think they are protecting the client or advocating for the client's independence when in actuality the client is truly impaired and lacks sufficient judgment to make such decisions. I have seen at least a handful of lawyers follow an impaired client's direction that led to disaster, financial abuse, and unnecessary litigation. The takeaway from this is to learn about impairment generally, to be alert in noticing possible signs of impairment, and to really listen if someone else tells you that the client is cognitively impaired. Ask questions about how the person reporting to you came to believe that the client is impaired. Take this into consideration. If you have any reasonable belief that the client may not be capable of making important decisions involving finances, suggest testing to get more data.

A psychologist or neuropsychologist should be involved in testing the elder to develop information that sheds light on the capacity question. The doctor who conducts testing on an elder regarding the question of capacity will also interview the elder. This process takes place over two or more sessions, depending on the issues at hand. The elder is seen on different days and asked some of the same questions both times. Answers are compared and conclusions are drawn according to standardized reliability and validity criteria established for such testing by the American Psychological Association.

Family may want to find an objective way to measure whether an elder has capacity to make financial decisions, particularly if they disagree with the elder's decisions. Family members themselves may be in disagreement as to the elder's capacity. Often, family members will urge or push the elder to undergo testing to prove that what they thought is true: namely, that the elder is impaired and should be stopped from making the objectionable decision. The elder may resist. Without a court order that testing be done, as in a guardianship or conservatorship proceeding, no one can force an elder to undergo testing. Without the testing, though, those in conflict on the question of capacity have little data and less help for reaching agreements.

Knowing how difficult it is for mental health professionals to pinpoint the precise extent of an elder's impairment, you can imagine how difficult it is for everyone else in the elder's life. Adding to this difficulty is the fact that some elders whose financial capacity is diminishing are unable to perceive that they are impaired; others are in denial about their impairment.

One concept those working with elders should be clear about is that some people who are cognitively impaired are not aware of this fact. The term used to describe this is *anosognosia*,[4] which refers to brain-cell changes that lead to a lack of self-awareness. For instance, a client could have serious memory loss and be completely unaware that he has any problem with memory at all. A simple way of looking at it is to say that the very part of the brain that would allow the client to perceive his deficits is impaired and he simply can't recognize the deficits. This is different from denying that a problem exists. A person with anosognosia really doesn't know that

---

4. http://alzonline.phhp.ufl.edu/en/reading/Anosognosia.pdf (last accessed March 12, 2015).

he has a defect, illness, or disorder. When this client tells you that things are absolutely fine in his life—even when they're obviously not—he really believes that they are just fine.

The Value of Objective Information

For any lawyer contemplating the representation of an aging person who presents with issues about mental capacity or diminished ability to make financial decisions, you serve the client best by insisting on getting objective information rather than merely relying on your own interview with the client. This is true for any professional who is contemplating having the elder make important decisions. That client may seem fine during social conversation but in reality may be unable to fathom the consequences of a legal or financial transaction. You won't be able to determine this just by talking with him once or twice. If anyone involved in the legal matter before you has raised the issue of capacity, it is worth doing the work of finding out why. As a mediator, I have seen too many horrible mistakes made by lawyers who lacked information about the aging brain, dementia, and diminished capacity and who created nightmares for others by relying solely on their own short-sighted judgments in deciding that an elder was "just fine." None of us can possibly know if someone of advanced years is "just fine" without making a concerted effort to fully explore the crucial question of capacity.

As a professional, you must not be fooled into thinking that you and you alone, with no input from family or anyone else, can positively determine your client's mental or financial capacity when doubt has been created by someone else or something outside your client's conversation with you. Warning signs that warrant your attention could include a forgotten appointment, a phone call revealing that your client didn't remember that you spoke to him earlier that day, or confusion in following the conversation you are having with him. Do not dismiss these incidents as "just old age." They are suggestions of memory loss, which can develop into dementia or be a symptom of dementia.

Litigation is not a prerequisite to getting the necessary interviewing and testing of an aging client done. If the family has not requested testing, and this is an issue, the elder's medical doctor can make a referral to the appropriate neuropsychologist or psychologist, or the family can seek out the expertise needed and request a referral from the elder's primary care physician. In some instances, the testing is sought by the elder himself, though this is less likely.

The significant cost of a thorough test series is an obstacle for some. Medicare does not typically pay for such testing except for a limited amount when it is ordered through a court proceeding. Resistance can also come from the person for whom testing is requested. She may fear "failing" the testing or having the true extent of impairment discovered.

Written summary testing reports can help you, as an elder's legal representative, to find out if your client is showing signs of diminished capacity at a level not visible to you personally. Although expert or specialist reports are no guarantee that others involved in a legal question with the elder will believe or accept the test results, I think it is better to use objective data to help you when a client appears to be in the "gray zone."

Accommodation for Diminished Mental Capacity

The elder does not have to be cognitively intact or even have testamentary capacity to simply be present for a legal proceeding. She may want to be there even if another person has been appointed her guardian or representative. The right and ability to make legal decisions is one thing. The right to be included and to witness what is going on is a very different thing and should not be overlooked. The lawyer may have to make a judgment call to determine whether it is appropriate for a cognitively impaired elder to be present in a court proceeding, conference, meeting, settlement discussion, or mediation. We can control how long the elder is present and for what portions of any proceeding. Accommodating the impairment includes recognizing that although the aging person may not be able to make a good decision or to fully understand, we demonstrate our respect for her by allowing her to attend and participate in a limited way.

Unless the lawyer is convinced that doing so is unwise and unhelpful, or the elder's disabilities are so profound as to make it impossible for her to participate, we encourage attorneys to include the elder to a limited extent in legal proceedings for as long as stamina and practical considerations allow. Even if a family member insists that the elder "won't know what's going on," we need to be aware that some of what is going on may just be getting through to the elder, despite her limitations. As mentioned in the description of "the gray zone," we can't be sure what part of a person is cognitively intact and what part is not. Therefore, we need to be cautious before accepting the characterization of an elder as totally unable to participate in any meeting, decision making, or proceeding.

The failure of others to fully recognize what an elder is capable of understanding, as well as common negative stereotypes, can affect how families, business professionals, attorneys, arbitrators, judges, and others characterize elders. Dismissive attitudes based on these stereotypes, if not addressed in some way, could preclude the elder's participation. A lawyer representing an aging, cognitively impaired client can advocate for the elder's participation; can set limits on how much and how long that participation will be; and can ensure protection of the client's right to be there if he wants to attend, no matter how limited his comprehension.

How Do You Decide Whether an Impaired Client Can Participate in Legal Proceedings?

The best way to make a decision about allowing a cognitively impaired client to participate directly in a proceeding (other than a deposition, which requires complete cognitive capacity to understand and answer questions) is to collect information, use a sort of mental checklist, and make a decision through a reasoned process.

For example, let's imagine that your client is impaired and a guardian has been appointed to speak for the client in your case. A settlement conference is set. The guardian can handle the matter competently. Should your client also attend the settlement conference? Family say, "He won't understand any of it, so don't bring him." Here are some things you can ask yourself and others to help decide whether to have your client attend:

1. **Objective information:** Are there any medical reports or testing reports of cognitive ability? If so, let that influence what you present to your client and what you expect of him. A designation of "severely impaired" would provide guidance.

2. **Current social ability:** Does the elder become agitated if he loses track of what is being said? You don't want to create unnecessary stress. Discussions at a settlement conference, even if all of the decisions will be made by the guardian, could overwhelm a vulnerable and easily confused elder.

3. **Stamina:** Would the elder be able to sit in a room for a few hours? Should she be accommodated and leave early? How would that be arranged? Discomfort from sitting too long or being unable to rest could aggravate impairments. Would the difficulty of getting to and staying at the conference outweigh the benefit of attending?

Accommodating Diminished Capacity by Limiting Participation

Participation of the elder may not include any decision making. It may mean simply attending a proceeding or conference without saying much. It may mean limited participation, when the elder makes only a brief, token appearance. It is a gesture of respect, even if the participation makes no visible difference to others there, and even if the elder never says a word.

To plan ahead for an aging client's limited participation in any legal matter or proceeding, you will need to think through the process and where your client might best fit in. Transportation will have to be arranged. A caregiver might need to be in attendance. This is a far cry from simply asking that your client show up at a certain time. You can provide guidance as to what time to be there, where to go, and for how long you believe it is appropriate for the elder to be present. You can rely on the input of those closest to your client for additional guidance and their opinions as to how to make it easiest on the elder. All in all, this comes down to a carefully considered judgment call.

Other Questions Beyond Objective Data, Social Ability, and Stamina

These are only suggestions and are not meant to be an exhaustive list of deciding factors. However, they may help you determine whether or not to include your client in a legal proceeding. If others say "no" but you think maybe you should include your client, consider more detail about her ability.

1. **How long will your client have to put forth effort?** Remember that attending anything includes getting up, dressing, eating, and using available transportation. These activities alone can tire out some frail elders. Would the proceeding be too physically demanding for the elder's ability? You will need input from family and/or caregivers, so consider this carefully. There is more to attending than being in the room. You do not observe the client's daily routine, so you will need to ask about capacity to participate physically, particularly if the meeting is to be held any distance from the client's home.

2. **Is the elder able to speak, hear, and understand the spoken word?** Some stroke victims, dementia-impaired persons, or those with other debilitating illness are unable to process speech. If the client's brain is affected to that extent, he or she cannot get meaning from others' words. This does not refer to a language barrier or those who may be able to understand speech though unable to form their own words. Rather, it refers to cognitive impairment of the ability to take in and process spoken information. We can't assume how well anyone does this without asking for detail from those close to the elder.

3. **Is the elder able to maintain alertness for several hours at a time?** This goes beyond stamina and considers the elder's ability to pay attention. Brain disease, medications, and other conditions can impair alertness. Essential medication can have side effects such as drowsiness, and the elder may be sleepy during the day. If she is unable to stay awake and attend to what is going on, there is no point in trying to make her sit there for hours at a time. Even in a person with adequate cognitive ability, physical and pharmaceutical factors can impair alertness to the extent that the elder's participation is not practical.

4. **Is the elder able to express himself to others?** An elder with cognitive impairment may not be able to communicate, either by word or gesture, his desires or preferences. Inability to express oneself by words or other nonverbal means can increase agitation and anxiety. We want to avoid frustrating the elder by placing him in such a position. If communication by listening and nodding is all the elder can manage, and he can do so calmly, that might be fine. If you put him in a roomful of

people when he can't say what he wants to say, you could be unnecessarily stressing an aging and communication-impaired person.

5. **Does the elder have any behavioral issues that would be stressful or disruptive for others?** Some persons with cognitive impairment, mental illness, or other conditions affecting behavior may exhibit difficult or disruptive behaviors in an unpredictable or uncontrollable manner. Shouting, profanity, removing clothing, inappropriate acts, and physical aggression are some examples of disinhibited behaviors that are seen in persons with brain impairments. If an elder has exhibited such behaviors, it is inappropriate for him to personally attend a proceeding. His voice is best communicated entirely by an advocate who is familiar with his needs.

General Mobility Issues

As an elder-friendly lawyer or other advocate, you may need to ensure accessibility to your office or any office where the aging person is to appear in person. In working with elders, we have to be much more aware of potential barriers, such as stairs that must be climbed or the kind of chair the elder may need. If the elder uses a wheelchair or walker, any meeting must be arranged in a location that is accessible with the device. If the elder has hearing loss or other physical impairments, we need to anticipate how best to accommodate these to permit the elder the greatest possible level of comfort and ability to fully take part in a meeting or conversation.

Things a younger person takes for granted may not work for a person of advanced age. For instance, if the matter involves an elder, we don't assume, without asking, that the elder is able to come to an office without assistance. If you are not sure whether your 95-year-old client can climb stairs and you don't have an elevator, you can simply ask, "Will you have any problem going up a flight of stairs?" I have had aging clients say "no"—and then I watched as they held onto a rail and half-dragged themselves up to my floor. Perhaps they don't like to admit being limited, or perhaps they think they just have to do it because there's no alternative. Sometimes it's easier to go to them if you know about mobility problems ahead of time. I offer this, and some take me up on it.

If you know that a client has mobility issues, be sure to communicate about the accessibility of your office and the availability of handicapped parking nearby. Those who work extensively with aging clients must get used to the idea that they will need to make home visits from time to time. It may limit you if you don't have the copier or other conveniences nearby, but documents can be mailed or emailed to your client after you complete your work.

Working with Physical Impairments

Hearing Loss

As diminished hearing[5] and sight[6] are common with advanced age, the lawyer serving aging clients must be conscious of these difficulties so that the elder's needs can be met. About 40 percent or more of the population over age 75 had hearing loss, as reflected by a report to Congress in 1986. By 2011, the percentage of older adults with hearing loss had climbed to nearly two-thirds of the population.[7] As our population ages, the percentage increases. Inquiring about hearing difficulties prior to meeting your client in person is a good first step but may not be sufficient. It is not unusual for people with hearing problems to minimize them out of denial or embarrassment. And don't assume that a hearing aid will enable a person to hear fully. Some kinds of hearing loss are not correctable with hearing aids. In fact, a hearing aid may create as many problems as it solves by increasing distracting background noise and distorting the source of sound.

Because so many people over the age of 70 experience hearing loss, I look directly at the elder and speak distinctly. I always ask, "Can you hear me okay?" Many people with hearing difficulty, regardless of whether they

---

5. U.S. Congress Office of Technology Assessment, *Hearing Impairment and Elderly People: A Background Paper* (OTA-BP-BA-30) (Washington, D.C.: U.S. Gov't Printing Office, May 1986).
6. Allen L. Pelletier, MD, Jeremy Thomas, PharmD, & Fawwaz R. Shaw, MD, "Vision Loss in Older Persons," *American Family Physician*, 79(11), 963-970 (June 1, 2009).
7. http://www.sciencedaily.com/releases/2011/02/110228090212.htm (last accessed March 12, 2015).

are wearing a hearing aid, do a bit of lip-reading to help them communicate. Facing a person when you speak can facilitate lip-reading and will avoid embarrassing the elder, or causing her to keep asking you to repeat what you said.

Another layer of this problem is that many people do not like their hearing aids or do not use them properly; they may lose or forget to wear them; or they refuse to get one, even if it is obviously needed. We just can't be sure. Consider the fact that Medicare does not pay for hearing aids. Some don't care to pay or can't afford the rather steep out-of-pocket cost. I test the waters by assuming that hearing might be a problem, and use a bit louder than normal volume with my voice. I ask if they understand what I'm saying at the outset and again as we go along. If they cannot hear, I either change where I'm sitting or speak up more. If a client's hearing is adequate, I don't change the volume from my normal speaking voice.

Remember also that even if a client can hear you, and has no cognitive impairments, her processing speed may be somewhat slower than a younger person's. Articulate clearly and try not to talk too fast. Don't let a few moments of silence make you uncomfortable; the client may be perfectly capable of processing new information and formulating responses if allowed to do so at his own speed.

Visual Impairment

About 1 in 28 U.S. adults older than 40 is visually impaired.[8] The risk of vision loss, like hearing loss, increases with age. Elders who have trouble seeing may not admit it and may feel embarrassed about the problem. They may avoid reading and paperwork. Legal disputes almost invariably involve paperwork—documents, contracts, instructions, reports, evidence comprised of written words—so we may take it for granted that clients can read what is handed or mailed to them. Because so many elders have some diminution in visual acuity or ability, it is *not* safe to make this assumption when working with elders, particularly those of very advanced age.

---

8. Allen L. Pelletier, MD, Jeremy Thomas, PharmD, & Fawwaz R. Shaw, MD, "Vision Loss in Older Persons," *American Family Physician*, 79(11), 963-970 (June 1, 2009).

Illustration of Visual Impairment Problem and
Accommodation: Diane's Mother
I was reminded of this recently when dealing with a dispute between an aging woman and her daughter, "Diane," about signing a durable power of attorney document (DPOA). There were numerous other contentious issues between them as well. The mother, age 84, was essentially housebound. She had not seen a doctor for several years, and could not get to a doctor due to numerous problems. Diane was trying to help change all this, but could not get her mother to sign anything. She had also given her mother a booklet (an American Bar Association publication) that I had provided about the importance of the health-care directive, but her mother had dismissed talking about it. They had an ongoing argument about the DPOA. I visited Diane and her mother at the mother's home.

I explained the document and the mother accepted that signing it was a good idea. But when Diane gave her the document, she pushed it away. In trying to figure out what was wrong, I then asked her what Diane could do for her to make things generally easier in her life. She gave me a list of what she wanted, which included "books on tape." That was a clue that she might have a vision problem. *Why would she need recorded books otherwise?* I wondered.

I asked her if she had any trouble with reading. She was not wearing glasses. She said that she did have trouble and wanted to go to an eye doctor for an examination. It was clear in this case that vision loss was adding to the problems between mother and daughter and had contributed significantly to the mother's resistance to the things her daughter was trying to get her to do. She was likely afraid to sign something she could not read, and had been unwilling to admit that she could not see the paperwork well enough to read it.

I asked if she would like me to read the paper to her, and she did want that. I read it slowly and explained each section. She agreed to sign the document. A notary who was on standby was called in to witness her signature. When Diane gave her the paperwork, she seemed lost; we both helped her find the appropriate signature line. When the notary asked her to sign his book, she again seemed lost. Her daughter pointed to the exact place to sign the notary book. Even Diane had not understood the extent of her mother's vision issues. Asking about the possible impairment and adjusting what we did helped immensely, and the problem was solved.

Accommodating Limited Activity Tolerance

An older person may be in excellent health and able to sit in a room all day if needed, just as a younger person might. But many cannot. Older clients tend to tire more easily than younger clients. They may have less energy for long meetings. Many elders take medications of some kind, and many take multiple medications. Often these have side effects of drowsiness, a need to use the toilet frequently, dry mouth, and so on. All the elder's possible difficulties should be anticipated when planning the length of any client meeting.

Arthritis is quite common with aging, and many elders have difficulty sitting in a chair for lengthy periods. I encourage them to stand, walk around as needed, or otherwise move about without having to ask if it's all right to do so. I offer frequent breaks, keep water nearby, and assume that most will need to take breaks during anything that lasts longer than an hour. This is especially true for depositions or other matters that can go on unpredictably for hours.

Illustration: Accommodating Limited Activity
Tolerance: "Virginia's" Deposition
In one matter, my 90-year-old, hearing-impaired client, "Virginia," was doing her best to get through an unnecessarily extensive deposition. I insisted on breaks every hour. I offered to walk her to the restroom across the corridor and some distance away. I made sure she had water at all times. When she hesitated, I asked her if she had heard the question. (No, she hadn't.) Ultimately, I insisted that the deposition be continued to a second session. I could see that Virginia was wearing thin and was exhausted, not only by being there but also by the unpleasant attitude of my opponent. I was able to advocate for her with her limited stamina. There was not much my opponent could do but accept the rescheduling of the rest of his questions for another day. I gave him a time limit and got up to leave when we reached it.

Being a good advocate for your aging client may mean being an advocate for more than the client's legal position. It should include the client's comfort, too.

Travel Considerations

Aging clients in frail health may not be able to travel the statutorily required distance to a deposition or other proceeding. If you are an advocate for an aging person, take into consideration how travel will affect your client. Considerate opposing counsel may be willing to work with you and accommodate your request to make things easier for an older person—but some may not. Those situations may necessitate motions or other means to help prevent unnecessary stress on your client. For a lawyer representing an aging person, there is a need to look ahead and figure out how to manage a situation in which travel is required. You don't want to find out on the day of a deposition set for a place 75 miles away that your client can't make the trip due to some physical limitation. You don't want to be surprised that your client can't attend a distant court appearance because of a limitation. *Ask*, arrange, and look ahead to best serve your client.

The use of Skype for communication via computer, or videoconferencing, if available, are creative options that can enable your client to participate without having to travel to some proceedings. You can suggest these if your client's needs or limitations make you aware that this would be a better choice than travel.

Conclusion

For lawyers who have not represented many aging clients, an increased level of awareness of possible age-related problems will help provide better legal services. We do not want to automatically assume that every elder is impaired; at the same time, we need to look for and expect that many of our aging clients will have some impairments, whether they admit it or not.

Anticipating, asking directly, and getting information from family and caregivers about the need for accommodation will assist you in keeping elderly clients more comfortable and better able to receive the benefits of your representation and advocacy.

3

Common Elder-Specific Issues

Introduction

In Working with Aging Clients, we may think we are doing a specific legal task, but then find that age-related problems either change our original intentions or cause us to be unable to carry on with the work that we were initially asked to do. We may find ourselves thrown into conflicts that have little to do with the reasons the client sought legal advice in the first place.

An awareness of the likely problems that many elders face over time will help us. We can be prepared with good and reliable community resources, and relationships with other lawyers specializing in areas outside our own skill sets to whom we can refer matters we do not want to handle. If, for example, we start out with a financial transaction and tax matter but find that family members are complicating the issue with things that are of concern to them, we may have to include another lawyer or other professionals in our efforts to serve the client's needs.

Life Events

Any client may be affected by life-cycle events, such as marriage, birth of a child, retirement, and other transitions. With elders, life transitions and losses associated with aging can profoundly affect your work and their participation in it. These transitions may be associated with a family member dying, changes in the family as a result of impairments of aging, and chronic illness. The list of issues can be quite extensive; here, though, we make an effort to touch on the issues most commonly encountered.

Whether your work involves real estate, business, personal injury, estate-planning, or anything else, when working with aging persons, you are likely to encounter questions that tend to be elder-specific. Aging itself raises issues that affect elders and, thus, any legal work you do with them.

Aging and Its Problem Areas

General subject areas that are likely to affect your work with an elder may include the following:

1. Whether the elder is impaired or not
   - Is the elder "normal," "just getting old," or impaired at all?
   - How impaired is the elder?
   - What is impaired and what is intact?
2. What rights to making general life decisions should be retained by the aging person and which should be taken away for the elder's safety?
3. General financial decisions
   - Can the elder handle the checkbook and pay bills?
   - Is the elder still able to make investment decisions?
   - Does the elder have complete financial decision-making capacity, or is she impaired in any way?
   - Is the elder competent to decide to give away property or items of value?
   - Should the elder be permitted to decide to give away assets of value as gifts?
   - Does the elder have the capacity to enter into contracts or transactions that have serious consequences?
4. Living arrangements
   - Should the elder continue to live alone, even though it seems to be unsafe? Does the legal work you do affect this?
   - Should the elder have the freedom to refuse help at home even when family members insist that it is necessary?
   - Should the elder have the right to encumber or sell the family home?
   - Where should the elder live if/when he runs out of money to support himself?
   - Should the elder continue to drive, or have the car taken away?

5. Elder abuse
   - Is the elder subject to undue influence?
   - Is a specific person in the elder's life taking advantage of or abusing him? Are you being drawn into a potentially dangerous situation by predatory family members or others?
   - Is the elder making unsafe financial decisions, to her own detriment?
   - Is the elder being harmed by another, either physically or emotionally?
   - Is the elder neglecting himself to the point where intervention is needed?

6. Testamentary capacity
   - Can the elder create a will and/or trust with your help?
   - Does the elder have the capacity to change a long-established estate plan?
   - Is the elder competent to change the durable power of attorney or health-care directive?
   - Is there danger to the elder who contradicts long-standing values and beliefs when she asks you to perform a legal task?

7. Romantic involvement
   - Does the elder have the capacity to participate in a romantic relationship or marry?
   - Does the elder have the capacity to consent to anything you are asked to prepare for her?

8. Caregiving
   - Who has the obligation to care for an impaired elder?
   - Does the caregiver have a right to compensation from the elder's assets?
   - What is appropriate compensation for caregiving?
   - Should the elder be placed in a care facility?
   - Does the elder have a right to refuse all care?
   - Who has the obligation to pay for care of the elder?
   - Is the elder eligible for any public benefits? If so, what will it take to get them?

9. Family dynamics
   - Sibling conflicts over care and responsibilities, and control over decision making and finances

- Sibling communication and expectations
- Parent/adult child conflicts and communication
- Parent/parent conflicts and other potential conflicts you may become aware of, even if they do not directly involve you as the attorney

10. End-of-life issues
    - Health-care directives
    - Medical treatment and hospice care
    - Withholding or consenting to care
    - Location of end of life and who decides location

11. Post mortem conflicts over estates and probate/administration of estates

Issues Surrounding the Cost of Caregiving

If an elder wants to remain in his own home, as most do, keeping the elder safely at home when he needs help can be tremendously expensive. Few people plan adequately and appropriately for this, despite increasing longevity. This is a source of ongoing financial pressure, not only for the elders themselves, but also for those who take responsibility for caring for them.

Most people pay these caregiving expenses out-of-pocket. The costs vary from state to state, but they are an expense that many people have failed to anticipate. Even if they have done good planning, many aging persons still run out of resources to meet their own needs due to their longevity. As people age, their families, professional advisors, and others in their lives may be thrown into conflict about the financial issues that aging creates. These costs affect the elder's own resources, and may require selling the elder's home, using up savings, depleting IRAs and pension plans, and selling off assets an elder may have intended to leave to heirs. Therefore, the elder's needs may deplete resources that adult children expected or felt entitled to inherit, thereby creating conflict.

Even if an elder in failing health and losing independence is not in an expensive care facility, she will still face significant expenses for caregivers at home, or for other care expenses that Medicare doesn't cover. When adult children are expected to step up and start paying for care or supporting aging parents from the children's own resources, disputes arise. Adult children may resent their parents for putting them in that position. Elders may resent having to depend on anyone for support; sometimes they don't seek care that they desperately need because they know they can't pay for it and they refuse to ask others to do so. Elders are frequently unprepared and embarrassed that they have not planned ahead or that they did not anticipate the high costs of their own needs. They may have refused to discuss financial matters at all with their adult children.

Because the high cost of caregiving is not usually paid for by any insurance (long-term care insurance is an exception), the financial pressure this creates is the source of many disputes involving elders and their assets.

Diminished Capacity Issues

The issues surrounding diminished capacity become more acute as disputes arise outside the question of testamentary capacity. The legal "test" for testamentary capacity does not require that the person be capable of managing all of his or her affairs or making day-to-day business transactions. As people live longer and more aging persons are affected by dementia, the question of capacity has become more of an issue. It affects not only an elder's decisions about day-to-day matters, but every aspect of the elder's business and legal affairs as well.

Loss of competency and capacity for decisions is often related to progressive disease processes, and the elder's decline in mental capacity may be uneven, unpredictable, and difficult to assess. Many of the common issues enumerated earlier derive from unclear answers to the question of whether the elder is impaired.

If, for example, an aging man wants to sell a business and you are asked to prepare the documents, a question could arise in your mind about the client's capacity to understand valuation and pricing as well as the transition associated with the sale. This is just one example of how an elder-specific issue can arise outside the estate-planning field. Any concern or uncertainty about the elder's capacity puts a burden on the lawyer or other professional involved to consider the ethics of the proposed transaction, regardless of how the professional might benefit from doing the work the client wants done.

Complexities of the Competency Issue

Every attorney and every business professional needs to understand that there is often no clear line of demarcation between a competent elder and one who is only partly competent or incompetent with regard to financial decision making. This issue can also arise in connection with any important decision. Although issues related to dementia are common, in my experience the competency issue is often misunderstood, even by the family members who are struggling with an elder who shows signs of memory loss or who has a medical diagnosis of a particular kind of dementia. Every lawyer who can or will represent aging individuals needs an understanding of the basics of this brain-destroying disease.

If you expect to work with aging clients or want to deepen your understanding of cognitive impairment, seek opportunities for more education on this subject, as it is only briefly described here. This is not meant to be a complete treatise on diminished capacity. However, this is a pervasive and growing problem; we can't escape exposure to dementia and cognitive impairment, whether it occurs in our own families or in our clients or both. We need empathy to grasp how hard it is on the persons affected with the underlying brain diseases that cause impairment and on those who love them and care for them.

How Can a Lawyer or Other Professional Tell
If a Client Has Diminished Capacity?

For purposes of this part of the chapter, we focus on diminished financial capacity rather than other kinds of capacity. A client may have impairments that also affect other life decisions, but perhaps the thorniest issues about decision-making capacity center on finances.

We may not be able to tell if a client's capacity to make financial decisions is impaired simply from meeting him and having a little chat. Your client or potential client may sound pleasant and be socially engaging. She may have a sense of humor. He may be able to discuss the latest sports or news events with you. But there is more to diminished capacity than meets the eye. Much research has been done in the area of loss of financial capacity by prominent researcher Dr. Daniel Marson, JD, PhD, a professor of neurology at the University of Alabama at Birmingham. Here I summarize some information provided by Dr. Marson,[1] based on his extensive studies, on the components of financial capacity, which he breaks down into nine domains. These are tasks a client would need to be able to do independently to have (or demonstrate) full financial capacity.

You might not have an opportunity to witness your client doing all of these tasks, but each of them is a marker of ability to manage finances and therefore to make financial decisions. A clinician can evaluate a client's capacity for these tasks in an effort to find out whether or not she is impaired. Even if you are not exactly evaluating your client, you can certainly inquire about her ability to do these things. You as a professional will need to make some determinations, particularly if your client seems to need a doctor's evaluation of capacity.

Domain 1: Basic Monetary Skills

This includes naming coins and currency, and understanding their values and relationship to each other (e.g., is a $5 bill worth more than a $10 bill)? Basic monetary skills will not be visible in your interactions with your client unless you are in a situation that would reveal something about him, such as going to lunch and paying cash.

Domain 2: Financial Conceptual Knowledge

Can your client define financial concepts? For example, does she know what a loan is? If you asked the client to explain a loan to you, you would know more about her ability to understand the concept.

---

1. Daniel Marson, "Impact of Dementia on Capacity to Manage Finances and Prevention of Financial Exploitation: The Aging Population, Alzheimer's and Other Dementias—Law and Public Policy," paper presented March 1, 2012, at the National Health Law and Policy Resource Center, University of Iowa, Iowa City, Iowa, nhlp.law.uiowa.edu/files.../Impact%20of %20Dementia-March%201.ppt (last accessed April 7, 2015).

Domain 3: Cash Transactions

Can your client purchase items at the grocery store, figure the tip for the wait person in a restaurant, or know what change to get from a vending machine? If you did go to lunch with your client, would you ask her to calculate the tip? That will give you some clue as to whether she can do it.

Domain 4: Checkbook Management

Does your client understand withdrawals and deposits? Can he use the register to track them?

Domain 5: Bank Statement Management

Can your client read and understand the financial statement when he gets it? Can he use it? If you go over a financial statement or accounting document of any kind with your client, you could ask him to reiterate what you said or give you some feedback. This does not mean that you ask a yes-or-no question, such as "Did you understand that?" You should draw out your client enough to see what he can demonstrate of his understanding in his own words.

Domain 6: Financial Judgment

Dr. Marson identifies this as one of the most important domains, and it will certainly affect any lawyer or other business professional working with an aging client. Financial professionals need to be informed about this domain. Can your client recognize a scam when faced with one? Can she identify mail or telephone fraud schemes? Ask him why he would or wouldn't accept an offer made on the telephone or Internet to purchase a real estate deal or other product that promised a high rate of return. Use an example and test her knowledge of what makes a deal phony or suspect.

Domain 7: Bill Payment

Can your client understand, prioritize, and pay his bills? One way to test this yourself is to ask if he has help from any family member or friend to do this. Does she pay her utility bills herself? Does she need anyone to keep track of her bills for her? How long has this been needed? These are ways to probe ability in this domain.

Domain 8: Knowledge of Personal Assets/Estate
Lawyers may be accustomed to asking about knowledge of personal assets when determining whether a client is capable of making a will or trust. Other professionals involved with a client's finances may not inquire whether the client knows what she has, including her real property and other assets not being managed by the professional in question. If you ask questions in a respectful way, you will be able to get a clue as to your client's knowledge. If she resists telling you, gets upset if you ask, or gets defensive, these are possible signs that she is uncomfortable with your questions because she can't remember or doesn't know the answers. People often get upset and defensive when they feel put on the spot and don't know the answer to a question. In contrast, a competent elder will be able to tell you, at least generally, how much he has in the way of assets, real property, accounts, and so on, and can give you at least a basic summary.

Domain 9: Investment Decision Making
This domain is most critical to probe and understand when a client is requesting to enter or is being asked to participate in a transaction involving an investment. Probing this domain can indicate whether your client has the capacity to measure and understand risk. Promises of high returns can be very seductive to an elder who is worried about running out of money. If you ask your client to explain the risk of any transaction or choice he is being asked to make, and he can't do so, it is a sign of danger. His capacity in this domain may be impaired.

As one can see from looking at the extent of the tasks involved in the broad concept of financial capacity, determining capacity is a complex matter. Lawyers must not assume that they know whether a client is impaired just from having a normal conversation with the client.

Note that keeping track of political issues or current events is *not* listed as one of the tasks that demonstrate financial capacity. Some people who can't add or subtract a deposit or realize that an Internet scheme is phony can at the same time be quite socially appropriate and talkative. Because the risk of financial abuse is a grave concern, bear in mind that an older client not may be as capable as he appears on the surface when it comes to financial judgment.

You, as a lawyer, financial advisor, or other provider of services in an older adult's life, may not be able to tell definitively whether or not your client is significantly impaired. However, spotting any red flags is critical. Once you know what to look for, you have a direction; if you recognize potential problems, you need to hold up your transactions with that client until you have further information. After you gather the necessary information, you are better prepared to act in an ethically appropriate way. Above all, if you suspect that your client is impaired regarding financial or other important decisions, do not just proceed as if everything were fine and do whatever your client tells you to do. If you carry out the instructions of a person whose capacity for financial decisions is impaired, harmful and even disastrous consequences can follow. Beware!

You may see these red flags in your client:[2]

1. **Memory lapses:** She forgets her appointments or calls you numerous times in a day, forgetting that she called earlier.
2. **Disorganization:** You asked your client to bring certain records to you, but he has been unable to keep track of them and they are all out of order, with some missing. It was a simple request.
3. **Math mistakes:** You go to lunch with your client and he is unable to calculate the tip.
4. **Confusion:** Your client can't keep track of what you are saying and keeps asking you to repeat it. You do and it does not help.
5. **Impaired judgment:** Your client tells you about some people he "met" on the Internet who promised a huge return on his money if he invests with them right away.

These red flags should be signals to you that your client may be developing a problem that will interfere with his judgment about finances or the business you have been called upon to do with or for him. Whether they are indications that your client is developing dementia or whether they are caused by something else is not something you can determine without outside help. It is important to have your own policy about how you will proceed if you

---

2. Marson, *supra* note 1.

see any of these red flags. Such a policy could include escalating the matter to another person to discuss your options, contacting a family member and comparing notes, or declining to proceed with business until your client has been evaluated by a doctor. The most important takeaway here is that red flags are indicators of possible trouble with your client's mind. You do not want to risk doing anything to endanger your client's financial safety by permitting business to go on as if your client had no problem.

What Is the Extent of a Cognitively Impaired Elder's Rights?

The elder's right to self-determination, to independence, and to the freedom to make decisions—even questionable decisions—is a starting point. From there, we address an elder's rights as they may be outweighed by the interest in protecting the person from harm. A reason why so much conflict arises about elders' freedom to make decisions is the tension created by the concern of both the involved family and the state to allow an aging person the freedom she deserves while at the same time protecting vulnerable elders from abuse, fraud, and the deterioration brought about by the changes of aging.

For example, a lawyer representing an elder, and advocating for the elder's right to choose whatever he wants to do, may clash with the family's concern that doing whatever the elder wants could leave him penniless or in physical danger. The family of an elder may try to take legal action to force the elder to do what they think is best. Unless the elder is not competent, he can make his own choices—to some extent, even unsafe or foolish choices. We hope that lawyers, physicians, and other advisors can persuade elders not to make foolish decisions, but some elders are unwilling to accept advice even from competent or trusted others.

Illustration: Doing Exactly as the Impaired Client Asks

In the case of Susan, Cynthia, and the financial advisor, discussed more fully later in this chapter, an advisor did exactly what his 95-year-old client asked him to do, without regard for the fact that his client was different from when he signed up to have the advisor manage his account. He had impairments and vulnerabilities. His client was being financially abused. However, the advisor just did what his client asked, even though he knew that the man was being manipulated by a predatory son. It took Susan, the elder's daughter, several months to get the needed doctor's reports, and to get herself positioned as successor trustee, to stop her brother's financial abuse of their father. In the meantime, the combination of a lack of clear policy on the part of the advisor; lack of direct guidance from the father's lawyer, to whom Susan had turned for advice; and the financial advisor's robot-like implementation of the impaired elder's requests could have allowed the predatory son to wipe out all of the father's remaining assets.

Older clients do have the right to self-determination. However, when professionals do not act appropriately to examine an elder's potential lack of financial capacity, the elder is put at risk for financial ruin. One can't always just do what the client says without question. We as professionals have an ethical obligation to keep our clients safe and to at least consider whether the client we knew years ago is still the same person now, given the advanced age and the potential for diminished capacity. If an aging person is a new client, whose history you do not know and whose life situation is also unknown to you, your obligation to get more information before you act only increases.

Other kinds of decisions besides financial ones can also be very difficult for elders' families. Adult children often do what they can to keep their aging parents safe, but when the elders resist, the children may not be able to stop their parents from making unsafe decisions. If an aging person is still competent, it is said he has "a right to his folly." A lawyer or other professional can advise and try to persuade a client if asked, but ultimately a competent elder can choose to do things that are dangerous or harmful. Such choices are not in and of themselves evidence of incompetence.

Illustration: The Right to a Dangerous Decision— Marina's Mother Living Alone in the Family Home

Marina's mother, Tatiana, who was in her early 80s, continued to live in the family home, a two-story house she had been in for more than 50 years. Tatiana constantly argued with her two daughters about staying there, despite the fact that she had had two falls already and her balance was poor. She had not been seriously hurt, but they were worried and even angry at what they saw as their mother's stubbornness. Marina and her sister believed that they had both a duty to prevent their mother from falling and getting hurt and the right to decide that she should move out of the family home. However, the mother was entirely competent. Mediation was offered, but the mother refused it.

Given that Tatiana had no cognitive impairment, she retained the right to make her own decisions. The house itself was not an unsafe structure, but the stairs were a problem. It was Tatiana's choice to keep using the stairs even with her dangerously poor balance. Unfortunately, Tatiana eventually did fall down the stairs and suffered a broken neck. Eight months, one surgery, and a lengthy rehabilitation later, she finally agreed to move out of the home at the insistence of her physician. Ultimately, she adapted well to her assisted-living apartment and was happy there.

Marina felt sad and sorry for her mother, but accepted that her mother had the right to choose this dangerous situation. Tatiana was not in imminent danger, as would have been required for a guardianship to be set up, and she was quite capable of telling everyone at the time that she did not want to move to assisted living, or anywhere.

This scenario is not uncommon. The elder's right to make decisions that others find questionable is an ongoing source of distress when they elicit fear in those who care for and about the elder. The more competent the person is, the less likely it is that anyone can take away his right to choose such things as where to live, how to spend money, and whom to associate with or marry. The more cognitively impaired the elder is deemed to be, the more likely it is that a court will intervene and limit the elder's freedom.

In working with elders, this is likely to be a recurring theme across the many kinds of conflicts a lawyer may encounter. If you are representing a stubborn client whose family is fearful for her safety, bear in mind that advocacy should be tempered with common sense. Sometimes we attorneys may forget that we are also *counselors* at law. The counseling part of our work can easily include persuading a stubborn client to consider the point of view of others and to look deeply at the safety issue families may be worrying about. Your voice as a lawyer or trusted other carries weight. A focus on advocacy and opposition does not always serve the aging client's best interests, particularly when the client's own judgment is impaired.

The Driving Dilemma: Should Lawyers Get Involved When a Client Is an Unsafe Driver?

No one wants to think about getting old, much less having to give up driving. If you know or represent an elderly client, you may hesitate to bring up the issue of driving, even if a client's family member has said he's worried about it. Should you bring it up? What if your client gets mad or tells you it's none of your business? This is such a personal issue, and it has enormous impact on the elder's independence.

The problem of older drivers who become dangerous behind the wheel is growing as our population ages. I think we have to remember this and consider our possible roles as professionals in the lives of our clients. We have an opportunity, in many instances, to influence the conversation about driving.

The subject of older drivers and safety is one with which I have extensive personal experience. For nearly three decades, I handled hundreds of injury cases, representing victims who were injured in auto accidents. Everyone ages differently, and many older drivers are safe to drive in advanced years. However, the older they get, the greater their risk of accidents.

In cases I handled where the accident was caused by an elder who likely should not have been driving, the situation was usually the same: The elder had no recollection of the accident or did not know what happened. This was true even in instances when both vehicles were destroyed beyond repair in the collision, the elder had run someone off the road, had run a red light, or caused another such memorable crash.

In one case, the elder had rear-ended the victim and pushed her car off the road and into a tree; he testified that the other driver had come at him and backed her car into his! Of course, this was impossible, given the position in which the police found both cars. His front bumper was smashed into her rear bumper, and her car was pinned to the tree by his car. The elder was so confused he literally did not know what he had done. Being confronted with the circumstances of the accident, as happened in a lawsuit, was just too much to face. He could not process the fact that his driving had caused a crash, so he invented a bizarre explanation.

For aging persons with impaired thinking, this is not an unusual scenario. Memory lapses, slowed reaction time, vision trouble, hearing loss, confusion, medication reactions, and other age-related thinking problems all contribute to making some elder drivers dangerous on the road. You could probably find a news report in any state on any day describing how a terrible accident or fatality was caused by an older driver who got confused or thought the accelerator was the brake. One such news report covered an elder driver who stepped on the gas instead of the brake, causing death and injuries to others. He survived and was interviewed. In his confusion, he stated that he had "lost control" of the car for reasons unknown. There is always something that cannot be explained, because the driver is unable to say what happened.

In 2003, 86-year-old George Weller killed 10 people and injured 63 others at a street market in Southern California by driving through "road closed" signs and wooden barriers. He showed no remorse when sentenced to five years' probation on 10 counts of vehicular manslaughter.

A 2006 study by the Insurance Institute for Highway Safety found that only teen drivers have a higher rate of fatal crashes than drivers aged 65 and over, based on number of miles driven. And because older drivers are more physically fragile, their fatality rates are 17 times higher than those of 25- to 64-year-olds.[3] Because the rate of serious accidents rises dramatically for the oldest drivers (those over age 85), we all need to be concerned. One might ask, where was the family of George Weller, who killed 10 people? Where were his doctor, his lawyer, and the others who knew him? It was not the first time he had gotten confused, according to the news stories. In all the other serious accidents involving older drivers, I wonder why no one in their lives took the step I am urging you, as a lawyer, business professional, advisor, or other influential person, to take. We collectively need to ask—and urge—these impaired folks to stop driving. It is for our own safety, as we are on the road with them too, but for public safety as well. Everyone around them is at risk.

Your aging clients might be among these dangerous older drivers. Lawyers can join the efforts of auto insurers, the American Medical Association, the American Association of Retired Persons, and communities to provide

---

3. "How to Help an Older Driver," https://www.aaafoundation.org/sites/default/files/ODlarge .pdf (last accessed March 12, 2015).

guidance to our older clients and their families on how to deal with the aging driver issue.

How We Can Help

I believe that any concerns you have about your client's driving should be addressed, not ignored. This is not always possible to do directly. Your client may be a difficult person. You may not know your client's family members. But if you have an opportunity, it is certainly appropriate to mention that you are worried about her or that you noticed that she got into a scrape in your parking lot and you want to talk to her about that.

Your comfort level in raising the topic with your client will depend on the kind of client you have and how amenable she is to your general advice. Some clients will be turned off; others will listen to you because they trust you and know you have their best interests at heart. For your more trusting clients, you can bring up the subject in the context of talking about other business, such as financial planning, estate-planning, changes in living situation, or travel. You might say, for example: "Jack, now that you're 85 and we've done [name task or business you've conducted], I wanted to get your ideas about how long you expect to be driving. I always want you to be safe and I wasn't sure if you'd considered what you might do if you couldn't drive at some point."

Note that the conversation starts with *your* concerns: that is, you want the client to be safe. This is always a good way to begin, as it does not immediately put your client on the defensive, as an accusation or telling him what is wrong with his driving might do.

If your kind and respectful approach doesn't generate a willing response, you might bring it up again later. If you know the client's family and can contact them about any concern you have, *do so*. I see no breach of any professional duty in trying to protect your client from harm. It's reasonable. Clearly you can't force her to talk to you about it, but if you never try, there is no chance of helping her.

It is important to be aware of how personal and emotional the subject of driving is for most people. In my own consulting practice, I hear families tell me too often that their elders refuse to stop driving even after losing their licenses. Some elders are reported to be so angry at their families' bringing up their driving that family warfare has been the result.

Families may need our help as professionals to reinforce their efforts. An elder with whom you have a trusting relationship in which you provide legal, financial, or other services may be persuaded to accept your encouragement to give up the car keys. This effect can be strengthened if you are echoing the urgings of family members or the client's physician to give up or reduce driving. We can provide resources, help the elder look ahead at alternatives for transportation, and generally be a source of guidance.

This subject should never be taken lightly. When an older person is faced with the possibility that he might have to stop driving, it can generate a strong response. The impact of losing the ability and right to drive can be devastating and life-changing. Elders may express outrage that anyone thinks they are less than capable. They may express fear of being cut off from all the activities outside the home that are meaningful to them. They may be angry that anyone wants to take away their freedom. They may see loss of this ability as a final blow to their independence and autonomy. But when they get the same message not only from their relatives, but also from the professionals in their lives, it may move them from resistance to acceptance.

Most elderly drivers decide to stop driving themselves. More than 600,000 drivers age 70 and older decide to give up driving each year, according to a 2002 study published in the *American Journal of Public Health*.[4] It's the other drivers, the ones who are unable to recognize that they are impaired, who are most concerning. It takes cooperation among all those who touch their lives to help them make this life-changing transition from total freedom to loss of independence with driving.

If you are seeking ways to justify bringing up the older-driver issue with your client, consider these ideas:

- You are a caring professional and you want the best for your clients. You do not want them to endanger themselves or others.
- You know your client, particularly if you have had a relationship over time. He has confided in you. He trusts you. You owe it to him to speak

---

4. "Older, Dangerous Drivers a Growing Problem," http://usatoday30.usatoday.com/news/nation/2007-05-02-older-drivers-usat1a_N.htm (last accessed March 12, 2015).

to him if you think he needs help with this important choice about giving up driving.

- Driving is a right and a privilege under the law for people who qualify. It has legal implications, so you are in a position to discuss the legal concepts of personal freedom versus public safety with your client and to educate her about her rights and duties.
- Our lawyer's Canon of Ethics allows us to take protective action for our clients. Though we are not required to do so in other contexts, why not do it in the context of personal safety? Bringing up the subject is taking protective action, as I see it. So is sending in a form to the Department of Motor Vehicles asking for reexamination, if it comes to that. Both choices are far better than saying "It's not my business" or that the problem belongs to someone else. It belongs to all of us as a civilized society.
- If you know your client is confused, has dementia, or has been diagnosed with Alzheimer's disease or anything else that clearly affects his driving, you don't want to be on the road with him. Protect yourself.

Tips for the Conversation About Driving

If you have an aging client who you think will listen to you and you are concerned about her driving safety, here are some ways you may be able to have the necessary conversation about driving.

1. Choose a good time to talk, preferably when the client is with you face-to-face. Remember that this is a delicate subject. Start with your own concerns first and then offer some observations that sparked your concern (e.g., you noticed that his balance is not good, his vision is getting worse, or he gets a little confused at times).
2. Give the client some information. Most people over 70 who have physical/memory problems do start by limiting their driving. Would she be comfortable giving up night driving to start with?
3. Offer to work with any available family to provide information and resources about driver safety, testing, and alternative forms of transportation in the area. Help your client think through how he could get around if he could no longer drive.

4. Give your client some written materials that you can download from the Internet on older driver safety. Some suggestions are listed in the Resources section at the end of this book.

5. If you are really worried, because your client has dementia or any other condition that puts him at obvious risk for driving, you may contact your client's family member with your concerns. Perhaps there is no family member or you do not know whom to contact. Most states have a means to report an older driver to the Department of Motor Vehicles (DMV) so that the state agency can request that the older driver be retested. In California, for example, a "Request for Driver Reexamination" form is available online.[5] You get the form, check the boxes with the reason(s) for your belief that the driver should be reexamined, and the DMV will send a letter to the driver requiring that she come to the DMV for testing. The dangerous ones will not be able to pass the test.

If you serve many aging clients and expect that the driving issue will come up repeatedly, it would be helpful to keep on hand some materials to offer your clients or their family members to help them address the problem of unsafe driving. See the Resources section at the end of this book for more on elders and driving.

Dementia and Its Effect on Financial Capacity

Financial Capacity Is Diminished Early with Dementia

Research on the subject of declining mental capacity, specifically to handle money, suggests that with Alzheimer's disease (which is by far the most common form of dementia), the loss of financial capacity happens early in the disease process, even in the very first stages. As discussed in Chapter 2 and earlier in this chapter, *financial capacity* refers to a person's ability to manage his or her financial affairs in a manner that is consistent with self-interest and personal values.[6]

---

5. https://apps.dmv.ca.gov/forms/ds/ds699.pdf (last accessed March 12, 2015).
6. Donna Pinsker, PhD, et al., "Financial Capacity in Older Adults: A Review of Clinical Assessment Approaches and Considerations," *Clinical Gerontologist, 33*(4), 333 (October–December 2010).

Studies have demonstrated that financial capacity is already significantly impaired in persons with mild Alzheimer's disease; in the moderate stage of the disease, all financial capacity domains are severely impaired.[7] Despite this, the elder may be functioning relatively normally in social settings. Conflict can arise because some elders may appear to be able to manage independently while in fact being extremely vulnerable to undue influence or predatory action by others regarding the use of or decisions about money.

In the early stages of dementia, an elder may seem independent, able to live alone or with an equally elderly spouse, and be able to drive or manage activities of daily living without assistance. Appearances are deceiving, as those who do not witness the elder trying to keep track of the checkbook, or spending, or investments may not be aware of any problem.

Family, friends, brokers, bankers, financial advisors, attorneys, and others may differ considerably in their perceptions of whether an elder is impaired at all, even with a diagnosis of dementia, because she can still keep house or pay the bills on time. Even in the face of considerable evidence, some people in the elder's life, even those in frequent contact with her, can be in denial that the elder is suffering from the effects of cognitive decline. Unfortunately, these elders are quite vulnerable to those who have profited from them or are trying to do so, who usually insist that the elder is just fine and is doing nothing wrong.

Financial Services Professionals and Elders with Cognitive Impairment

Financial services professionals and those who may be contacted to carry out questionable decisions by aging clients can be caught in the middle with little guidance. Confidentiality restrictions can cause them to act on an elder's wishes without checking whether a family member knows of his or her impaired capacity. Financial professionals to whom I have presented this legal issue consistently express concern that they cannot discuss an elder's financial matters with anyone, particularly adult children, due to regulatory agency and legal requirements of confidentiality.

---

7. D. C. Marson, S. M. Sawrie, S. Snyder, et al. "Assessing Financial Capacity in Patients with Alzheimer Disease: A Conceptual Model and Prototype Instrument," *Archives of Neurology,* 57(6), 877-884 (2000).

Those in a fiduciary relationship with aging clients may feel bound to carry out an elder's demands because they have no clear way to stop the elder from acting in a way that appears to be contrary to his best interests. I suggest that all professionals dealing with aging clients rethink these policies. As our population ages and people live longer and longer, our traditional ways of dealing with "the average person" have become outmoded in many ways.

Illustration: Susan, Cynthia, and Their Father's Financial Advisor

Susan called in distress. She described her father, 95 years old, living in another state in a nursing home. He was frail, easily confused, and had memory-loss problems. Susan had been appointed to become her father's successor trustee for the family trust, as her mother had passed away some time ago. Susan had not taken the necessary steps to make the transition from her father being trustee to her assuming that role, but she was thinking it over and had talked to her father's trust lawyer. She and her sister, Cynthia, were worried. Dad had a close relationship with their brother, Johnnie, but Johnnie had always been manipulative of Dad. The latest development in that relationship had prompted her call to me for guidance.

Susan reported that she had gotten a call from her father's long-time financial advisor, who said he was calling her "on the QT," meaning he thought he wasn't supposed to be talking to her. He knew that she was her father's agent according to a valid durable power of attorney, but somehow he wasn't clear about her authority now, as Dad was supposedly still competent. Except that he clearly was not. Dad had been brought from the nursing home to the advisor's office by his son. Johnnie, who did not have a job, had flown in to visit Dad from Johnnie's home state thousands of miles away. Susan was used to paying for plane tickets for Johnnie, as she wanted him to continue to visit their father, who had always enjoyed the company. At their meeting, Johnnie prompted Dad to ask the financial advisor for a cashier's check for $50,000 and a credit card for Dad's cash management account, which contained all of the remaining trust assets. The total in that account was about $400,000. Dad had no other assets, though he did have a good income that paid for his care in the nursing home.

The advisor responded to this by doing what his client told him to do, even though he realized that Johnnie was manipulating his client; the advisor even told Susan this in his "QT" phone call to her. The advisor must have thought that call would somehow fix the likely financial elder abuse he saw taking place. He told Susan that he would "drag his feet" on getting the credit card, but after three months of delay, he obtained the credit card for the father—who couldn't even dress himself, much less go anywhere to use it. Fortunately, Susan had the card mailed to her address. I advised her to destroy the card.

Susan and Cynthia asked for advice about this problem. I directed them to act promptly to get their father evaluated by two doctors, as the terms of the trust required for transition to the successor trustee. That meant flying out from their two different states to meet with their dad and get him to two different doctors for evaluation. Fortunately, he was cooperative and the evaluations were finally accomplished. (Some elders are not cooperative, and every lawyer who drafts a trust for anyone should be alert to this potential problem.)

A few weeks later, Susan had the necessary reports in hand, verifying that their father was no longer competent to handle his affairs. After she got the necessary document (certificate) verifying that she was now the successor trustee, I directed her to inform the financial advisor in writing that her father was no longer competent to make financial decisions and that he was not to take any direction from his impaired client. She also provided the advisor with a letter from one of the doctors who had evaluated her father. That action cut off Johnnie's access to the cash management account and protected her father's remaining assets.

Meanwhile, Susan was able to access Dad's bank records. She found that Johnnie had likely manipulated Dad into transferring another $20,000 into a bank account from which Johnnie had already withdrawn most of the money. The next step was a firmly worded letter to Johnnie, letting him know that Susan was now the trustee and that any and all transactions pertaining to her father's trust assets had to go through her. Johnnie's abusive letters and emails were probably going to increase, but he had no money to fight any legal battle with her, and I expected that Susan would be able to keep her father safe from further manipulation by her brother.

What alternative steps could the professionals in this example have taken?

1. The trust lawyer, learning from either his own impaired client or the client's family members that the elder was in cognitive decline and at risk for financial manipulation, should have clearly instructed Susan about the urgency of getting the necessary doctor's reports to enable her to take over as successor trustee. He did not do so. He failed to treat the matter as a high-risk situation. Further, in the effort to draft a trust in the usual way, he did not consider what might happen if the client he represented refused to see two doctors for evaluation of his mental capacity, or what alternatives he had for drafting this portion of the trust so that a vulnerable elder would be protected from abuse while the lengthy process of making doctor visits and getting reports played out. Alternatives in drafting do exist. Clients who develop dementia are vulnerable to abuse because they often do not understand why they need to see any doctor, let alone two or more, or they flatly refuse to see doctors for evaluation because they are being actively manipulated by someone who says "It is a conspiracy. Don't go." This is not uncommon.

2. The financial advisor knew full well that his client, at age 95, was not in the habit of making large cash withdrawals nor of transferring money into different accounts. His organization failed to develop any proactive, senior-specific policies to anticipate and address the likelihood that some older clients will develop dementia and suffer impaired financial capacity. He failed to escalate the matter to any supervisory person or committee to determine whether it was prudent to suspend all transactions until Susan got the needed confirmation of his client's incapacity and could give him the legal document that would allow him to refuse to take direction from his impaired client.

Sadly, this is not such an unusual situation. We are perhaps all a bit less prepared, in our professional habits, than we could be for the rising tide of people living to be 95 or older, as Susan's father was. We need to think through the possibility that any client who lives a very long time may become impaired for financial decision making. We need to keep our documents and policies clear and be sure that they cover the resistant client who has dementia. We also need to develop new, senior-specific policies that allow for waiver of privacy and confidentiality when a client becomes vulnerable to financial manipulation.

Imagine the irritable older client calling his lawyer, stockbroker, real estate agent, or financial advisor and demanding some action that is an abrupt change from the elder's prior, long-standing habits of dealing with business or finances.[8] Imagine the struggle the service professional goes through in trying to fulfill the duty to the client while still trying to keep the client safe. The risk of being found liable for allowing a known dangerous or highly questionable transaction to take place is entangled with the responsibility to honor the client's instructions.

Such conflict-prone situations with elders are likely to become increasingly common. As the incidence of dementia rises, more financial transactions with impaired elders are taking place. There are no clear guidelines for anyone in such a situation that absolutely direct the right thing to do. Lawsuits by relatives of the elders and heirs, or potential heirs, claiming financial elder abuse by professionals are likely to increase with the aging of our population. Inevitably, there will be differences of opinion as to the elder's capacity or level of impairment.

Common Financial Transaction Issues

The following is only a partial list of financial transactions that may raise questions about an aging person's financial capacity in particular, or the elder's level of impairment:

- Risky investments or apparently inappropriate investments
- Disposal of the elder's assets
- Management of the elder's investment portfolio
- Unusual or significant purchases late in life
- Charitable donations made when the elder is in need of expensive care and cannot afford to make donations

---

8. *See* http://www.aginginvestor.com/dementia-how-to-protect-elderly-clients.

- Timing: appropriateness of a transaction for a person of the elder's age
- Who, other than the elder, makes decisions about the elder's finances, and when this power passes to that person
- Prudence of the successor trustee, durable power of attorney agent, executor, or other with financial management responsibility who is still taking direction from the elder
- In any transaction, departure from the elder's long-standing expressed beliefs, values, habits, and patterns of financial conduct

Lack of Clear Policies Specific to Elders

Financial institutions seem to lack the policies needed to address an elder's financial impairment until cognitive losses are extreme and very obvious. Advisors and managers may be unaware of how to spot signs of financial capacity impairment in a client. Not wanting to lose an account, advisors and other professionals may continue to accept direction from a long-standing client, even if they suspect that the client is in cognitive decline.

I perceive that we are at the beginning of a rising tide of disputes based on such scenarios. As our population ages, many elders will need care from facilities and must sell their homes and move. Property may have to be sold to pay the high costs of long-term care. Predatory and unscrupulous professionals may commit crimes of opportunity by taking advantage of the elder who needs to conduct a significant financial transaction. Because of the diminution of financial capacity and impairment of judgment, the elder is at risk for being significantly disadvantaged or abused.

The Effect of Financial Elder Abuse

Persons over the age of 50 control more than 70 percent of our nation's wealth.[9] Severe impairment in capacity to make financial decisions makes many older persons vulnerable targets. Predators may feel that frail elders will not live long enough to take legal action or that they will not make

---

9. http://www.preventelderabuse.org/elderabuse/fin_abuse.html (last accessed March 12, 2015).

credible witnesses.[10] Hence, financial elder abuse is a widespread and often underreported problem.

Current estimates put the overall reporting of financial exploitation at only 1 in 25 cases, suggesting that there may be at least 5 million financial abuse victims each year.[11] The annual financial loss by victims of financial elder abuse is estimated to be at least $2.9 billion, a 12% increase from the $2.6 billion estimated in 2008.[12]

A more recent study conducted by True Link, a financial services company, reveals that seniors lose $36.48 billion each year to elder financial abuse—more than 12 times what was previously reported. Their study showed that the highest proportion of these losses—to the tune of $16.99 billion a year—comes from deceptive but technically legal tactics designed to specifically take advantage of older Americans.[13]

When financial elder abuse has occurred, we are also likely to see more efforts to place cognitively impaired elders under guardianship or conservatorship. Elders who do not see themselves as impaired may vigorously resist. Those who can make a good appearance before a judge and who are socially appropriate may still be unable to safely handle their own finances. Along with everyone else, courts struggle with the difficulty of deciding whether or not an elder deserves to lose his or her freedom to guardianship.

The issue of elders' ability to make safe financial judgments when financial capacity is impaired in any way is very appropriate for mediation. The flexibility that mediation permits in working out compromises for the elder is an advantage over having a court make hard-and-fast decisions regarding issues that are often quite unclear and therefore have unpredictable outcomes. Elders are likely to need the opportunity for creativity that mediation can provide.

The following example describes an exceptionally complex financial abuse matter involving an elder. It involved a partially competent man, an

---

10. *Id.*
11. John F. Wasik, "The Fleecing of America's Elderly," *Consumers Digest* (March/April, 2000), cited in "National Center on Elder Abuse Fact Sheet" (2005), *available at* http://www .ncea.aoa.gov/resources/publication/docs/finalstatistics050331.pdf (last accessed April 7, 2015).
12. *The MetLife Study of Financial Elder Abuse*, 2 (June 2011); *available at* http://www .giaging.org/documents/mmi-elder-financial-abuse.pdf (last accessed March 12, 2015).
13. https://www.truelinkfinancial.com/research (last accessed March 6, 2015).

incident of abuse, a risk of further abuse, a family conflict over the elder's right to make all decisions, and numerous social issues as well. Lawyers were involved in questions about this gentleman's capacity from the beginning. His case covered a myriad of interconnected issues in estate-planning, real estate, probate, elder abuse, family law, civil rights, guardianship, and financial capacity.

Illustration of Diminished Capacity: Harold's Dispute

Harold, age 87, was recently widowed and very lonely. He was victimized almost immediately after his wife died by a female "friend" who simply took advantage of his generosity and his isolation by offering to move in and take care of him. He gratefully accepted. She told him she loved him, but explained that she needed financial help with a six-figure debt. Harold offered to pay—and did pay—her debt, much to the shock and anger of his adult children. She left shortly after he did so.

Over the next six years, Harold began to develop some memory-loss problems. However, he still paid his own bills, met with friends, and lived independently. His memory loss worsened, but he was socially appropriate, even charming. He met a much younger woman and fell in love.

Almost immediately, a family dispute arose. His adult children were furious, sure that his new, younger girlfriend was just another predator. They hadn't spoken to Harold for a long time, even as the relationship with his girlfriend continued. They had no plan to try to work out anything and threatened to have him put under conservatorship (guardianship).

However, due to his intelligence, independence, and socially successful interactions, it seemed unlikely that anyone would be able to prove that Harold didn't know what he was doing. Harold was angry with his "ungrateful kids," to whom he had given financial gifts in the past, for their interference in his personal life. This was a matter the family and Harold wanted to resolve through mediation. Harold had already sought advice and paid three lawyers to advise him about various aspects of these problems.

When we met Harold, we were not so sure he was fully competent to participate in mediation, based on the premediation conversations with his adult children. We requested that, for the sake of all, he undergo testing to screen for competency to attend mediation. Both a basic mental status examination and dementia screening were done.

Test data revealed essentially that Harold was capable of participating in decision making at mediation. The more in-depth kind of neuropsychological testing needed to determine financial decision-making capacity was not done at that time. (It was needed later, and more comprehensive testing did in fact occur).

There was evidence that the younger girlfriend was indeed after Harold's money. At the same time, she seemed to have affection for him and was taking good care of him. She was attending to him better than he had been attending to himself. He was happy, and he said that he wanted to be in a long-term relationship with the new girlfriend.

The purpose of mediation was to explore mending Harold's relationship with his children, as he was quite determined to get married again. His children were aware, having sought legal advice, that they would probably not succeed at efforts to have Harold declared incompetent by a court.

In order to bargain with them, Harold agreed, at the mediator's suggestion, to use a licensed fiduciary to help with at least some of his financial transactions. That was helpful. Although he was open to suggestions at times and intractable at other times, he was able to make a fragile peace with his adult children, who finally accepted the fact that he was going to marry his girlfriend.

The saga continued as lawyers became involved with his prenuptial agreement, his estate-planning, and other aspects of his life going forward. This entire picture was very complex, as Harold had impaired judgment regarding complex transactions; at the same time, though, he was clear about what he wanted and unwavering in his resolve to get it. He was certain about marriage, he talked to several lawyers about it, and never changed his mind over the next two months of discussions.

Eventually, he did marry his girlfriend. The adult children resented it. He did acquire an attorney to represent him at mediation and that attorney continued to watch over his financial affairs. His children were unhappy with his choices, as his new wife was going to be entitled to part of his estate. However, he prevailed in asserting his right to make his own decisions about his marriage.

Harold's dispute illustrates many of the financial capacity and decision-making issues involving elders. Harold's condition is also a good example of how difficult it can be for anyone to decide when it is safe for a partially impaired elder to proceed with financial decisions. His right to self-determination was at odds with an apparent need for protection. The limits on either of these necessities were never fully clear to anyone involved.

Mediation resulted in Harold's children agreeing not to stand in his way if he wanted to get married again. The surrounding complexity of addressing the administration of his estate, which had never been done after his first wife died, remained problematic. He had retained the power of appointment over his estate. His children didn't want him to completely disinherit them, which could have happened if at least some work were not done to reach agreement about the numerous issues beneath the surface.

Harold was hearing-impaired and kept losing his hearing aids. He was socially appropriate, and could be respectful and polite in conversation. However, he was highly suggestible and vulnerable in many ways. Three other psychologists besides the one who tested him prior to mediation later got involved. One tested him to be sure that he could enter into a prenuptial agreement; he was determined to be competent enough for that. One tested him to determine his capacity to change the estate plan to give certain amounts to his new wife; he was also determined to be competent enough to do that. A third tested him to determine if he could enter into complex transactions relating to the further disposition of his cash and real property; the outcome of that testing was not available to me at the time of this writing.

Despite doing well on some parts of the testing, Harold was advised by two of the psychologists that he should stop driving as a result of their findings. He agreed to give up the keys, though this had not been an issue prior to the testing. His new wife took on the role of caregiver, watching over him, driving him around, and addressing his memory problems.

Harold was quite capable of making some financial and other decisions, but was significantly impaired in other respects. His case demonstrates the cloudy nature of determining financial capacity and the nuances of decision-making capacity. The dilemma of his partial competency required three different attorneys, multiple sets of tests, a fiduciary, at least one mediation, and an ongoing effort to protect him from further predatory actions.

Harold's case involved real estate, family law, estate and probate litigation lawyers, together with an array of psychological experts. Although it was helpful, mediation certainly did not resolve this entire situation. His attorney was well aware of the dichotomy between Harold's apparent social competence and his vulnerability to the influence of others. This illustration may be an extreme example of how complex and intertwined these elder-related issues can become, but it is worth remembering.

Conclusion

No matter where we encounter our aging clients, and no matter what kind of work we may be asked to do with or for them, aging-related issues can arise. The more we understand these issues, the better we will be able to deal with them, and to provide competent advice for the elders in our practice and those who accompany them. We may regard the age-related problems discussed in this chapter as "someone else's problem," but the truth is that they are everyone's problem. Knowledge about and compassion for impaired clients and their life situations will make each of us better lawyers.

Early loss of financial capacity can lead to financial abuse before the elder herself even realizes that she is impaired. With an understanding that loss of financial capacity is inevitable and certain with those who have diagnoses of dementia, lawyers can and likely should serve as a resource for referrals as well, to appropriate experts who can assist aging clients and families get as much help as possible with these unclear issues. Likewise, any business professional in any capacity who works with aging clients needs a roster of vetted experts to whom a client can be referred for evaluation when doubts about decision-making capacity arise. Knowing your client's long-standing values and beliefs is helpful because it may reveal a change in patterns of conduct. Families of our aging clients need to be connected with competent other professionals as well, including neurologists, geriatric psychiatrists and psychologists, mediators, social service professionals, and community resources, such as the Alzheimer's Association and the local Agency on Aging. Every professional can at least provide suggestions and direction for those who first notice signs that an elder's capacity may be diminished.

4

Communication with Elders

Introduction

Good communication with elders is much like good communication with others, except that elders have unique characteristics that may demand a higher degree of effort. Impairments of the elders' senses affect their ability to communicate with lawyers, and require that we recognize and accommodate their impairments. In addition to the basics of communication skills and recognition of impairments, however, there are generational differences between some lawyers and their elderly clientele. Age-related social characteristics are addressed in this discussion.

As a lawyer, you will often be viewed as authoritative, even if the client or a family member acknowledges that their question is not the kind that you usually handle. They want to know what to do, and you are seen as someone who may have answers. Even if the subjects that come up have little apparent relationship to your specialty area of legal work, you may be asked about them anyway, just because you are a lawyer.

This discussion is meant to guide any lawyer in any area of practice to become aware of how to address common questions affecting elders in a competent way, with deeper awareness of how aging affects communication. Sensitivity to age-related questions can permit you to be of better service to elders and their families. You may refer the matter that the client raises to someone else who you think is better equipped to work on the particular issue, but the way you treat the elder is also important. No one wants to feel dismissed or ignored, especially when the topic is emotionally loaded.

Here are some ideas to help increase your understanding of and comfort level with aging clients.

These same ideas apply to financial and business professionals as well. You may have a long-standing relationship with your client. You may know him better than some of his other close contacts. In the context of your relationship, it is essential that you recognize age-related changes in your client so that you can continue to be of excellent service. What elders need as they get older changes from what they needed when they were younger. Accommodation of our aging clients covers not only how we help them to be physically comfortable but how we help them understand us comfortably as well.

"The Handshake Generation"

Attitudes and beliefs are part of any successful communication, and age-characteristic attitudes may surface in your work with elders. Being prepared for them can help you anticipate what tack to take or when to tread lightly. Although every elder is unique, there are usually some traits that tend to be common among those who are age cohorts in every generation. We shouldn't automatically assign a stereotypical trait to anyone, but we can look for things that come up repeatedly in a particular age group to help us communicate better.

Attitudes About Finances

For instance, elders who are over 75 at the time of this writing lived through the Great Depression and two World Wars. They come to us with some age-related traits shared by many others who had the same highly impactful experience. They have been referred to as the "handshake generation," meaning they tend to be trusting and at times naïve in some respects. For this reason, predators find them relatively easy targets, and issues of financial abuse (as previously discussed) are widespread.

The Resistant Spender

Many older persons who survived extremely tough economic times are frugal; very cautious about spending money, even on their own needs;

and seem somewhat shocked at the high cost of goods and services. Getting elders of this generation to spend money on help they appear to need is often a source of irritation and disputes with their adult children. This reluctance may extend to hiring an attorney to assist with a transaction, do estate-planning, or consult with when advice about any legal matter is indicated.

As an example, one of my clients, who was involved in a dispute with her daughter over moving to assisted living, seemed obsessed with the cost of paying for the assisted-living facility. She and her husband, both in their mid-80s and in frail health, had several million dollars in cash assets, in addition to a high-value home. In meeting with me, she reiterated that she wanted to get a certain public benefit and wasn't going to move until she did. However, because of her high net worth and cash assets, she would never qualify for that public benefit. She is not unlike many others we see, who have the means to pay for whatever it would take to keep them safely cared for, but don't want to spend what they have. As in this case, conflicts arise around the need to spend money for any kind of professional or other services as these elders lose independence.

Generally, beware of any client who is so resistant to parting with money that she spends a lot of time questioning why you charge what you do for your services. Vigorous arguments that you charge too much may be a hint that at the conclusion of your services, she will not be willing to pay your bill. I recommend either getting your fees in advance or avoiding this kind of client and declining the work, no matter how attractive the fee may look at the outset. You cannot change a deeply held attitude or belief about money with your logic about the value of your work or a clearly itemized bill. For an elder with this attitude, it is an emotional issue that ignores and overrides logic.

The Careless Big Spender

Other elders who have accumulated wealth may be big spenders, perhaps compensating for the deprivation of their earlier lives. As their needs change, they may be very resistant to reining in their spending habits, thereby creating a shortfall as their needs increase, as well as friction with those in their lives. There is a real risk that this elder will run out of money. Taking over control from an out-of-control spender is a common source of conflict between elders and their families.

The big spender who has always had enough but is going to deplete her assets if she keeps it up can be particularly difficult and resistant to advice. This elder may be unwilling to face the reality that she will have to pay large amounts for caregivers to help attend to her increasing needs as she ages. There may be a cognitive problem that the aging person is not even aware of. There may also be a problem with those who have given to good causes for decades but can no longer afford to do so; they may want to be generous and not understand that their circumstances now impose new limitations on charitable donations.

Secrecy About Finances

Some elders are very secretive about their finances, even with close family members. If a client or potential client has financial issues, it is best to ferret out the elder's attitudes about money at the beginning of your interactions with him. This will enable you to be tactful in addressing the elder's attitude about finances in general and the problem for which he or a family member seeks your help in particular. In any face-to-face meeting with a client who is older and has a Depression-era attitude about the subject of financial secrecy, it can be helpful to say that you will reveal as little as possible about his finances to others. This can help assuage the client's desire for secrecy—but be careful not to make any promises you can't keep. You may indeed find it necessary to discuss his finances with family or other professionals, such as a CPA.

Just learning what an elder's financial resources are and where they are located may be difficult; this is often the reason attorneys become involved in a dispute. In the example given previously, in which the daughter was trying to get her parents to move to assisted living, the parents had never had a conversation with their daughter about their assets. Until her father fell and had to go to the hospital, leaving a very disabled spouse at home, the daughter did not know if her parents even had any assets, let alone what form they were in, where they were kept, where the legal documents were located, or any other essential information. Even in the crisis period when her husband was hospitalized, the mother was still reluctant to share this essential financial information with her daughter, regarding it as a secret.

The Difficult Elder, Resistance, and Control

Aging, dementia, and their detrimental effects on the body and the mind can cause some individuals to become extremely difficult. Some elders were always difficult, and those behaviors do not diminish with age unless the elder makes a concerted effort to change. With elders who do not have brain disease, it has been my (wholly unscientific) observation that those who were easygoing and pleasant in their younger days seem to grow more so as they age and become infirm. Those who were difficult and unpleasant at an earlier time in their lives seem to become increasingly unpleasant with advanced age. I have never been able to truly explain this, except to note that with age, many elders become less inhibited and thus perhaps become less interested in monitoring or controlling their underlying ways of relating to others.

It may be a totally different story for an elder with dementia. The onslaught of the disease process can radically change an elder's behavior from how it habitually was prior to the onset of disease. Behavior changes with dementia are as unpredictable as loss of cognitive ability. No one can be sure of what will happen next. A sweet and patient older lady can turn into a grouchy and demanding person, and vice versa.

How the person used to be is of little consequence when we meet an aging client who needs legal work done. We simply have to take the person as we find her, regardless of descriptions given to us by family members or others about how she used to be or how she "really" is. Our ability to connect well with aging clients is based partly on our skill and partly on our patience, empathy, and compassion. These are all communicated primarily in nonverbal ways, whether or not the elder is entirely cognitively intact.

For those whose lives did not turn out as they expected or hoped, aging can be particularly trying. Anger, depression, and its accompanying irritability, oppositional behavior, and other symptoms can make it very hard for professionals, family members, and caregivers to move the elder forward in making decisions.

Fear and Resistance

Sometimes, the threat of losing one's independence can cause an elder to become extreme in resisting help. This may happen even when it is obvious to those around him that he really needs help and is unsafe without it. This is a frequent source of conflict among aging parents and adult children. We handle this by continuing to acknowledge the expressed resistance from the elder; for instance, "This must be very hard for you to think about, now that your son will be managing the family finances." Continued recognition of the elder's resistance and reiterating and summarizing it can make an interaction go better with an elder of this mind-set.

Communication About Giving Up Control

The transition of power and control over the checkbook from aging person to successor trustee or agent with power of attorney is often a communication challenge. Families may try to get an aging parent to resign as trustee before forcing the issue, especially when the elder already shows some impairment regarding financial decisions. However, an elder may not want to lose the status of being the decision maker, as she has always been. He may not see the need for him to resign or change anything. He feels fine, he will tell you. Continued respect and recognition of the resistance are important in this situation as well.

Communicating with Depressed Elders

Depression among elders is not uncommon. Elders may suffer many losses besides decline in their mental and physical abilities. Loss of spouses, family members, and friends is inevitable as people age, and can contribute significantly to the incidence of depression.

Depression can directly affect your interactions with your client. One of the characteristics of depression is difficulty in making decisions. Other symptoms can include resistance to change, negative thought patterns, sadness, and feelings of helplessness and hopelessness. All of these can contribute to difficulty in moving forward with the work you have before you. For example, if you need a client to review and approve a document you have drafted, and he doesn't get back to you, depression could be a factor. If the aging client or a family member mentions that he is feeling low, or seems depressed, or you expect depression due to a life event such as recent loss of a spouse, it can be helpful to find out what your client is going through that makes it hard for him to follow through with what you need him to do. It is especially useful to find out if the elder has seen a physician for treatment. Without appropriate treatment for depression, it can be extremely difficult for elders to take next steps that may have been agreed upon, thus undermining your good work.

Fortunately, depression in elders is treatable. Positive results are often seen with a combination of medication and talk therapy. Despite the availability and positive effect of medication and therapies, elders may be unwilling to seek treatment, embarrassed at the perceived stigma attached to seeking mental health help, or unable to comply with treatment recommended by a doctor.

The generation we presently consider elders is not a "therapy-savvy" generation. The culture in which our elders grew up was not one that valued or trusted in psychotherapy for help with emotional problems. The result may be that we have a high number of untreated mental health conditions among elders, as compared with the general population. I often hear clients say things like "My mom is so ill mentally, but she won't go see anyone." It is helpful for the lawyer to understand this problem, as it may take persistent and frequent follow-up or face-to-face meetings with your client to get anything done.

The elder's physical decline, isolation, or other mental health issues can cause those around them to react badly or try to impose restrictions. Caregivers may become angry or frustrated. Lawyers may find their depressed aging clients uncooperative or apparently unwilling to follow through on advice or recommendations.

We cannot repair the effects of depression on our aging clients, but we can offer empathy, an understanding ear to hear about the elder's difficulty in making a decision, and encouragement to keep trying. If we have the kind of relationship with the client or a family member that would make it acceptable to suggest getting a checkup from a doctor, given the circumstances you have observed, by all means suggest it. We cannot and should not pretend that the problem doesn't exist. Lawyers in a position of authority as professionals may have a positive influence on clients and families. Our kind words and informed suggestions can make a difference in guiding a client to get help from other professionals when help is needed. Some elderly people respond very well to medication to treat depression, and they get through the stressful events with less emotional pain. It is an outcome worth trying to influence when you can.

Common Triggers of Resistance

Resistance to change, especially personal change, is also a recurring problem in elders. Fear is generated by suggestions to give up the familiar. Loss of physical and mental capacity causes some elders to feel vulnerable and fearful that if they change anything, they will lose all control over their lives.

Others in the elder's life may want him to make changes that the elder refuses. Sometimes family members want to know if there is a way to force the elder to make changes. The changes that families usually want were listed in the previous discussion about common elder-specific issues. Here we detail them further.

1. Getting Help at Home

Because social isolation poses risks to elders' well-being, both mental and physical, family members may want to bring help into the place where the aging parent lives. Some elders feel that this is an invasion of their privacy, and they don't want strangers in the house. Others refuse because of the cost. Others resist for a combination of these things and the fact that, to them, acceptance of help is a signal or admission of decline. Decline triggers fear of "being put in a home," of losing control over other aspects of life, or of the end of life. Acknowledging the fears associated with resistance and giving the elder ample opportunities to speak about them can be very helpful in addressing the issue with an aging client.

2. Moving Out of the Family Home

Family members or others may want the elder to move to another location or senior community when he or she loses the ability to manage activities of daily living independently. The elder resists moving, resists help with disposition of possessions, or resists the "intrusion" of well-meaning family members into the elder's daily life.

Efforts to move an elder to a different residence frequently trigger a family fight. The elder may be pushed into moving into a care facility against his or her wishes by well-intentioned adult children. Elders' fear of losing their home or sadness at the transition from all that was familiar may never be acknowledged. Again, even if the move is inevitable and necessary because of health declines and inability to manage alone, elders need to be provided the opportunity to speak about how it feels, to express their fears, and to vent any annoyance or anger with those who "made me do this." An understanding lawyer can be a safe sounding board. Even if your work involves reviewing the facility contract or other legal question, there is no reason you can't acknowledge how hard a move will be on the elder, along with doing competent legal work to protect the elder from any questionable clauses in the contract.

3. Taking Over the Finances

The elder may have made unwise financial decisions or have been preyed upon because of isolation, depression, or the inability to resist pressure, also called *undue influence*. When faced with the prospect of loss of independence about financial decisions, elders often experience anger and grief. For men particularly, who were most often the sole or primary breadwinners in this generation, the feeling of vulnerability can be overwhelming. It can be helpful for the lawyer faced with this kind of dispute to offer suggestions as to how the elder can be kept informed of all financial matters even if he is no longer in control. Even his symbolic inclusion in management of his finances can convey a sense of respect and aid in overcoming the elder's resistance to ceding actual control.

Other resistance triggers exist for elders, depending on their health and needs, such as the request to give up the car keys. At any point when there is a loss of independence, it is normal to encounter resistance. In communicating with elders about this, it is very useful to ask basic questions about how they feel. Because some elders are not in the habit of talking about emotions—which may be a characteristic of this elder generation—they may not have much vocabulary for verbally expressing their feelings. Lawyers can help by asking leading questions and by learning that most basic of communication skills, listening without interruption. We can also encourage elders' efforts to put their feelings into words.

Confidentiality and Elder Abuse

In communicating with an aging client or in dealing with their families in any context, a suspicion of elder abuse could arise. There may be subtle signs, or an elder could reveal it directly. Because elder abuse causes financial losses of more than $2.9 billion per year,[1] our chances of encountering it in our dealings with elders are significant. We may not be mandated reporters of abuse as other professionals are, such as doctors and caregiver agencies, but that does not preclude us from reporting abuse. However, we are bound by confidentiality in our client communications, and this can be an obstacle to some lawyers who consider it off limits to report what a client tells us. However, if we have a reasonable suspicion that a client may be in danger financially, physically, or otherwise because of abuse, I believe that our ethical obligation in most situations is to reveal the suspected abuse to the local adult protective services organization.

Our duty to our client's safety may supersede our duty of confidentiality, but this is an ethical judgment call for the lawyer. The ABA Model Rules of Professional Conduct state that "[a] lawyer must always be sensitive to the rights and wishes of his client and act scrupulously in the making of decisions which may involve the disclosure of information obtained in his professional relationship."[2] In my view, this does not mean we look the other way or give a pass to anyone who is suspected of abusing, unduly influencing, or otherwise taking advantage of a vulnerable elderly client. When in doubt, I will ask a client if he is aware

---

1. *The Met Life Study of Elder Financial Abuse*, 7 (June 2011); http://www.giaging.org/documents/mmi-elder-financial-abuse.pdf (last accessed March 12, 2015).
2. ABA Model Rules of Professional Conduct, Canon 4 (a lawyer should preserve the confidences and secrets of a client).

of a situation that to me appears suspiciously like abuse. Sometimes the client does not see the harm. Sometimes a client may be too intimidated to speak up, but the lawyer comes across evidence of another's conduct that could or does put the aging person in danger of some kind. Sometimes the client is fearful of retaliation. One must consider all the circumstances before deciding whether to report potential abuse. Will there be retaliation, and would the client be worse off if you report what you see? My own conscience does not allow me to refrain from taking protective action for a client, and I have reported suspected elder abuse. I have found that when a lawyer contacts Adult Protective Services, the report does carry some weight. We know how to gather facts, describe issues, and provide necessary detail. The only thing that could stop me might be a client who is adamant that she does not want the suspected abuse reported. In that situation, I might be left with the choice to withdraw from any further work on the client's behalf. If you have a client in an apparently abusive situation who insists that you not report it, I would recommend respecting the client's wishes, but also acknowledging that it is too ethically uncomfortable for you to continue and putting your reasons for withdrawal in writing to the client.

Summary: Top Ten Pointers for Successful Communication with Elders

Ethical dilemmas aside, we can summarize some pointers to facilitate communication with aging clients. This list is largely based on my personal observations and direct work with many elders in various situations, both as a health-care provider and as a lawyer. These pointers are clearly not needed with every elder. Some appreciate our work and some do not. Some are impatient and want it done yesterday; others like a slower pace. Some take the changes of aging in stride, and others resist and complain. I generalize from my direct experience, as I have not found anything in the scientific-study literature that sums up these thoughts. These are some techniques that I personally use, given in the hope that you may find them helpful.

1. Embrace a Client's Appreciation When You Can

Many elders are more appreciative of our efforts to assist them than their younger counterparts are. I can't explain why this is so, but in working with elders over a period of years, I have definitely felt more appreciated by this cohort than by people of younger ages. It's a plus. I can speculate that their decades of life experience lead many of our elders to be grateful for the efforts of those they know are trying to be helpful. They're likely smart enough to understand that not everyone is trying to help. If they see your effort and are thankful, you may hear about it. So, enjoy the appreciation when you get it. I hope you will also appreciate yourself for making any extra effort it takes to work with an impaired aging person. It can test your patience at times!

2. Measure Your Pace

I have found that if we slow things down to a pace that is comfortable for a person with some impairments, things work fine. For example, if an elder is walking from one room to another, be conscious that you need to walk slowly with her compared with your usual pace, so the elder does not feel left behind, rushed, or embarrassed at being unable to keep up. There are notable exceptions, but I try to be conscious of this as a basic courtesy.

The same applies to the rate at which we speak, ask questions, and deliver suggestions. Think about not overloading a senior with too much information, explanation, or legalese at once. Some elders take a little longer to process what is being said. This may be part of their normal aging or due to various declining physical and mental abilities. I am conscious of the pace of a discussion and prefer to err on the side of going slower. In any event, I do not normally find elders asking me to hurry it up.

3. Consider Hearing Loss

Because hearing loss is so common with aging persons, expect it. We described this in the discussion on impairments, but keep it in your mind for all aging clients. Remember to ask about it. Test it out for yourself by asking if your elderly client can hear you. Look directly at the elder when speaking. Even a slight hearing loss will make it harder for them to get all the information you are trying to communicate. They may be embarrassed to keep asking, "What did you say?"

4. Don't Mention the Lack of Devices the Elder Might Need but Doesn't or Won't Use

We may wonder why an older person won't wear a hearing aid, or use a cane or walker or other assistive device. Bear in mind that most of us don't want to admit we can't do something on our own. Is it Yankee independence, a cultural value? I'm not sure. I do know, from long experience, that many elders just don't like hearing aids (it distorts the sound, it's uncomfortable), walkers (such a clunky nuisance), canes (I'm fine if I hold onto the wall), or wheelchairs (that's for "old" people). These things can mark them, in their own minds or in the minds of society, as debilitated, devalued, and useless or helpless. They don't like the feeling that engenders. I think it's best to remain tactful and make no comment about a client's refusal to use an assistive device, even if a family member brings it up ("Dad needs a cane but he's just too stubborn to use it!"). As my 92-year-old mother-in-law, Alice, recently put it when asked to please use the walker, "I don't want everyone to think I'm a cripple."

5. Take Bathroom Breaks Often

Many older men and women need to use the bathroom more frequently than younger people do. For men, this may be due to the common problem of enlarged prostate, or to the use of medications such as diuretics, which help control high blood pressure. They may need to excuse themselves from the room more than once an hour, but certainly more often than a younger person usually needs to do. The same can be true for aging women, for different physical reasons or from use of other commonly prescribed medications. I try to offer breaks more often than I would with a younger clientele, to seat the elder closer to the exit nearest the bathroom when possible, and to simply be aware of elders' potential needs.

6. Ask for Feedback Frequently

I try to stay very conscious of the rate at which an elder takes in and processes information by asking frequently for feedback. I ask if what I said was clear, and if the client has any questions, comments, or suggestions to add to the conversation. It may indeed be a normal part of aging that we process incoming information more slowly than a younger person. Assuming that processing might be a bit slower is safer than assuming otherwise. This has nothing to do with overall intelligence. It's just that it can take longer for the elder to fully understand. This is certainly not true across the board. I've met 90-year-olds who could come to a conclusion or do math in their heads faster than much younger people. However, it never hurts to test the waters by asking for feedback.

7. Invite the Elder to Express His or Her Thoughts

I have also found that many elders seem somewhat hesitant to speak up for themselves, or to take a strong position against the views of those who are in charge in their lives. This is clearly not true for every elder, but it appears to be true often enough that I feel the need for vigilance to be sure the elder's voice is heard and enough time is allowed for the elder to express her view if she is accompanied when you meet her. Extra effort to draw out the shy, hesitant, or easily intimidated elder may be called for. The habit of politeness may, for some elders, mean waiting until everyone else has finished speaking before they say anything. That could be never unless you step in and be sure the elder is specifically and directly invited to speak.

8. Consider Your Environment and the Client's Physical Limitations

If it is not your habit to work with those who have physical impairments, you must raise your consciousness about this in any regular work you do with elders. Accommodate an elder who has *any* physical trouble, not just those in wheelchairs. Note that not all bathrooms are wheelchair accessible, even if there is an elevator that makes the building itself accessible. Quietly offer help if an elder is struggling with a heavy door or other barrier. Sometimes even accepting help with such simple things can be a sign to an elder that he is not capable, and he will refuse assistance. Sometimes you can disguise such help as deference to a valued client, thus making it agreeable—or at least acceptable.

9. Remember Eye Contact

We communicate a lot by our facial expressions, and especially eye contact. For any elder—cognitively impaired, physically limited, or not—the ability to communicate in addition to our words is particularly important. Even if someone misses some of our words, or doesn't understand all of what we say, or gets confused, our eye contact can convey an anchoring sense of reassurance. "I'm listening to you," it says. Hearing-impaired people are especially helped by this. Show your attention by your facial expression and be particularly conscious of how often you use eye contact with your older clients.

10. Use Touch Judiciously

A handshake, a hand on someone's arm, or another brief gesture of physical contact can be important to an aging person, especially with one who has sensory difficulty or cognitive impairment. Again, it is a way of communicating warmth and reassurance that you are listening and that the person is important to you. Touch can have a very positive effect. At the same time, for some individuals, being touched is frightening or confusing. The more you learn about the elder, the more you will be able to judge whether touch is helpful to this particular person. Ask those in his life if the elder responds well to a handshake. That's a clue. One other thing to remember: Most aging persons have arthritis, which can cause a handshake to be painful. No hard squeezing! I offer a gentle, light handshake to any elder.

Conclusion

All of these measures may be useful some of the time, and some will be needed most of the time in working with elders. Everyone ages differently. There are nonagenarians who are athletes. Some people over 100 years old are still mentally sharp. And don't be surprised if you meet a spry elder who needs no accommodation, tells you to get on with it, and otherwise busts every stereotype you've ever held about aging persons.

5

Elders and Family Conflicts

Introduction

Issues with elderly clients most often involve families, or the elder's estate disputed by families. Hence, a broad spectrum of issues affecting family dynamics comes into play. Most lawyers are not usually trained or educated to understand or work with the complexities of family dynamics. However, the skills necessary to be successful in working with your older clients' families can be learned. You may also find yourself representing a family member who is in conflict with an aging parent or other relative, and you will need the family dynamics skills there as well.

In this chapter, we consider our role with families, the various kinds of families and family dynamics we are likely to encounter, and some of the typical kinds of family disputes we see. We have to see each client in the context of where the dispute arose. If the legal matter is connected to others, there is no escaping the need to try to resolve it by interacting with other family members, whether represented or unrepresented.

Family Law Provides a Model for Collaborative Practice

My own bias in favor of a collaborative approach to representing elders will certainly come through in this writing. As an elder mediator, I witness devastating conflicts within and among families, some of which cannot be helped by mediation, as they are far too deeply entrenched. However, for others, the problems facing elders can often be worked out successfully with their legal representatives if the focus shifts from fighting to working collaboratively.

We have a successful model for collaborative practice in family law. Family law has many features in common with elder-related disputes, because they both involve families, highly emotional conflicts, and an opportunity for the lawyers involved to either work toward settlement or keep the fight going endlessly, driven by the high-conflict relationships. Clearly, from the mediator's chair, I see that the collaborative lawyers have greater successes and better outcomes for the aging individuals involved. I also see that aging clients are relieved of an unnecessary stress level that must be maintained if legal battles are continued.

The Lawyer's Role

We see many dysfunctional families. Their communication failures may be an essential cause of the conflicts they bring to lawyers in the first place. We must understand first that we cannot be therapists and fix all the ills that families may present. We have to focus on the present legal issues, and on the need to see if resolution is possible in advancing our client's interests. Whether family members reach the point of having better relationships as a result of our efforts to represent a family member, or they choose to keep fighting after the case is over and never speak to one another again, we acknowledge that it is the family's choice either way.

Although our job as advocates may bring us face-to-face with some of the worst and most dysfunctional families, we can also vastly improve communication and problem resolution in families. We may play a key role in urging our clients toward resolving the dispute, whether at mediation or in informal communications with opposing counsel. There is always the possibility that a family in conflict can reach a level of peace.

Some of the ugliest and most painful disputes are those that pit blood relatives or those related by marriage against each other. In this chapter, I suggest some strategies for deepening your understanding of family issues with elders and for facilitating efforts to get your case resolved before everyone's relationships are destroyed as a result of the legal process. Underlying conflicts among family members may have existed long before your tele-phone rang. In such a situation, the present lawsuit or proceeding simply becomes the most recent manifestation of a deeper mistrust or dysfunction.

Antecedents of Conflict in Families

When working with aging persons and/or their relatives, it is helpful to keep in mind where the conflicts about elders most often arise. These are the areas of money, division of assets, and paying for care of an elder. Many other issues about safety, shared responsibility, power, decision-making authority, and control also arise. End-of-life decisions are in another cat-egory; though such decisions are time-limited, these situations are fraught with heavy emotion that can result in highly contentious family conflicts. Lawyers can easily be sucked into these emotion-driven issues. Proceed with caution. If the real engine driving the case is emotion, a client is unlikely to be satisfied with a legal result. The family dynamic should be addressed when you see it, and the client should be made aware of what you observe.

To accomplish this, the lawyer first needs the skill to observe, question, and determine the extent of what is driving the case, and then the ability to develop a strategy on how to achieve a good result. Consideration of a good result must go further than thinking about how to overcome the opposing point of view or how to beat the other attorney. It must start with a focus on the elder in the matter, whether or not you represent that individual. Does this sound contradictory? You have an obligation to represent your *own* client. Yes, and your client probably exists, in many situations, in the context of relatives with whom he is having a dispute. The resolution of the dispute may involve much more than your taking a vigorous position on a legal principle. It may well involve how the elder's life going forward will be shaped by what you do. I urge every lawyer dealing with cases in which elders are involved to develop a sense of the whole: to consider the life of the aging person and to think through the effect your work will have on that life. It is entirely possible to be an excellent advocate while being a considerate human being toward all the parties involved in a legal matter. I will reiterate that many elders are vulnerable and should not be treated the same as any party on the other side of a case. It may be a shift in consciousness to think this way, but I encourage it.

Focus on What Is Best for the Elder

Family disputes about elders often involve adult children. When adult children are called into action to care for their aging parents, the primary focus ideally should be on providing the best for the aging parent. Unfortunately, because of long-standing issues and mistrust between and among siblings, that primary focus may become clouded and compromised. The sabotage of focus on the elder's welfare and safety occurs via expressions of hostility from family member against family member. These easily escalate into lawsuits when "hot-button" issues of finances and control are involved.

The emotional baggage families bring into intrafamily lawsuits is a unique challenge. Even when the elder is not present in your office, having adult children, siblings of the elder, spouses, ex-spouses, stepchildren, and others all speaking for the elder can greatly increase the complexity of reaching agreements.

We need to understand the undercurrents and the history that may motivate clients' behavior. We need to represent our clients vigorously, yet see the larger picture surrounding their concerns. If the underlying dynamics are ignored, the legal case can easily become a means of acting out personal issues. Litigation of the matter you are asked to become involved in may not serve the aging client or his family members in any productive way. When these matters get out of control, assets can be steadily depleted while the family fights on and on, never producing a truly winning outcome.

Lawyers I have observed sometimes seem oblivious to the overall harm their involvement brings to the family's disputes. I encourage a step back to consider how the lawyer can serve more as a peacemaker in these ugly family cases. Invariably, making peace is best for the elder.

Consider a Family's History

Resentments going back for decades can come to the fore when power and control issues are at hand. The kind of parent the elder was may also become an issue: not all elders were good parents.

Physical, emotional, or sexual abuse may be part of the family history. Likewise, we often see issues of neglect, mental health, life-threatening illness, and alcohol and chemical dependency as factors in family and elder disputes. All of these will color the parties' perceptions and their willingness to make agreements or compromises. They may color your own perceptions as well. These biases tend to appear when a family member is describing why she wants representation, how "unjust" the situation is, and how bad the other person involved may be or has been.

The family member who consulted you in the first place will look to you for advice. Should they file a matter in court? Is there any alternative? Although it appears that some attorneys are motivated only by fees, I like to think of the lawyer's role as that of a professional and wise guide for the client. From what I observe, protracted litigation of intrafamily disputes involving elders is rarely good for the elder. Not only is it extremely stressful for almost anyone to be involved in a legal process in the first place, the pain of opposing one's own relatives (by blood or marriage) can be devastating and ruinous to an elder's health. Many elders face physical and emotional challenges to start with, outside of the legal disputes, and the added stress of battling family can break down their ability to maintain their health.

Part of your skill set in dealing with a family dispute about an elder should include asking about the "back story." How did your client get to this point? What is important to her? What does he expect to accomplish in the legal case that is proposed or under way? In representing elders and their family members, competent attorneys need to do more than think of themselves as hired guns. We are capable of litigation or representation in any regard, but we are not dealing with a clientele that necessarily has the ability to fight without serious and sometimes irreparable harm to the most vulnerable participants.

I write this as a lawyer who had a long litigation career as well as a mediator who sees elder disputes from different angles. I can only urge those who are called upon to represent elders to consider how much harder the already difficult process of a legal battle is on a person with limited stamina, physical difficulties, perhaps some memory problems, and more of life behind them than in front of them. I constantly see lawyers make mistakes by drawing clients into legal fights that could have been resolved much earlier than the point at which they finally get settled.

Illustration: Muriel's Case

Muriel was 87 and had lost her husband three years before I learned about her. Her daughter, Rachel, had sought legal advice about her mother, who seemed to be losing her capacity to make competent decisions. First, after her husband died, Muriel had become less and less able to run the family business that she and her husband had had for decades. Rachel had occasion to look at the books and was horrified to see that her mother was unable to account for more than $300,000, apparently stolen by employees; the business was essentially bankrupt. Worse yet, Muriel had fallen and needed care. Muriel's sister and niece, living some distance away, offered to take Muriel in while she recovered.

The sister, Rita, had historically taken advantage of Muriel's generosity and had gotten large cash sums from Muriel as gifts over the years. Rita's daughter did not have a job, was not doing well in her life, and had often persuaded her mother to ask for money from Muriel to help her out.

Muriel had savings and owned a home that she was not able to maintain very well. Rachel had done a lot of work to keep it up. Rachel was the only child and was successor trustee as well as the agent named in Muriel's durable power of attorney. She began to take control of the assets and secure them, as she was sure Rita would try to get financial control when Muriel went to stay with her. She wanted to protect her mother from ruin, as it became apparent that soon she would have to pay for care for Muriel from Muriel's remaining assets.

Sure enough, Rita began to interfere with Rachel's efforts to protect Muriel. Muriel had early dementia and was readily subject to Rita's influence. Rita hired an attorney to try to undo all Rachel had done to protect Muriel. The attorney she hired did not know Muriel well but apparently thought that Muriel was quite able to make all her own financial decisions.

Although I consulted with Rachel early in the case, and it was handled out of my geographic area, I had enough ongoing contact with Rachel to learn what happened over time. The matter was referred to a local attorney for Rachel, who resided in a different part of the state. Litigation ensued. Eventually a compromise was reached and an independent trustee was appointed, but not before the relationship between mother and daughter was essentially destroyed; Rita and her daughter had, with their lawyer's help, pitted mother against daughter perhaps forever.

I question the actions of the lawyer Rita hired. He failed to look at the big picture. He did not consider what was best for Muriel, who had only one daughter and had previously had a good relationship with her. Getting Rita to control the finances was his goal, which may have been ethically questionable to start with, considering the family history. He never discussed the matter with Rachel before deciding whether to get involved in the fight. He apparently ignored the psychological reports that described Muriel's dementia. He did not consider the question of undue influence by Rita over Muriel. He simply collected his fee, drew battle lines, and exacerbated a conflict that could have been worked out long before it was actually settled. It is a scenario I see all too often: the lawyer who represents a family member does not consider the impact of the case on the elder herself.

Alternatives to Engagement in Family Disputes About Elders

At the very outset, a lawyer who is consulted about a case involving a family dispute has a unique opportunity to consider something other than increasing and protracting the conflict. There is a chance to ask many questions that will shed more light on the issues. Most often there are emotions driving the dispute, and the client or prospective client may not see the true underpinnings of the conflict.

Of course, as a dispute resolution practitioner, I believe that most matters can and should be mediated. If you yourself are not a mediator, you can increase your awareness of how an outside, neutral person might be of help in getting matters resolved before they devolve into ugly and protracted litigation.

Here is an example of a family dispute about an elder that did not escalate into a lawsuit. It is followed by an example of a different scenario that was not resolved. Imagine the lawyer's role in both situations.

Illustration: The Fight of the Three Sisters

Three sisters in their 50s, all living in different states, were reaching the boiling point over the care of their father, who was in his 90s. He lived in his own home and had dementia. The sister who lived nearest to Dad, Betty, was a professional, but had a somewhat pushy and controlling demeanor.

Her other sisters, Jennifer and Clara, were close to each other, and neither of them trusted Betty. In fact, their mistrust of Betty had gotten to the point that they wanted to sue her for what they thought was "mistreatment" of their father and failure to disclose certain medical information about him. They accused Betty of elder abuse.

If they had gone to an attorney who saw this as a great fee generator, that lawyer might have taken on the matter and filed a lawsuit, based on a lot of assumptions presented by Jennifer and Clara. Damage to everyone might have resulted. Betty lived close enough to her father to check on him daily, which she was willing to do. If they had gotten more polarized or Betty had been prevented from seeing him, Jennifer and Clara would not have known what was going on, and they would have had to pay a professional to give daily reports about their dad.

Dad was wealthy, and a fiduciary had been agreed upon to handle his finances. Fortunately, she saw the benefits of mediation and suggested it to the sisters, who agreed. In the various telephone meetings that encompassed mediation, Jennifer and Clara learned that Betty hadn't actually done anything out of line. Though they were tentative at first, they learned to trust her judgment about what their dad needed. They learned to communicate more effectively by having Betty send daily texts regarding Dad's status to everyone.

Because of mediation, they got along much better, and their father did not have to become embroiled in any stressful contact with any of them. It was a period of peace. Several months later, Dad died unexpectedly. The last part of his life was not marred by sibling warfare; instead, the sisters could concentrate on helping keep him safe and happy.

Illustration: Another Family and the Lawyers' Role: Two Against Two—Fighting Over the Parents' Home

This example illustrates a role the lawyer took, and the resulting distress of family warfare.

In this instance, two adult siblings, Rick and Sharon, had taken a position opposing their other two siblings. They were locked in a fight about how their parents' remaining, though limited, assets should be spent. Rick and Sharon were represented by an attorney who advised that Rick, who had rightfully and appropriately stepped in as successor trustee, did not have to listen to his other, disempowered siblings about how finances were handled and could do as he wished. After all, Rick was in charge and his lawyer was going to do everything to protect his right to make all independent financial decisions. His one loyal sister, Sharon, went along with this.

Both parents had dementia. The only thing they had expressed was that they wanted to remain in their own home. They were aware of the arguments among their adult children.

The other two siblings, Jake and Marta, were totally agreed on their position and totally polarized against Rick's exercise of power. He was making dumb decisions, they thought, and their parents were going to run out of money if he kept it up. Rick wanted to fix up their house, as one day it would have to be sold and it had to be repaired first. Jake and Marta wanted all the money to be spent on caring for Mom and Dad, and put off worry about the house until later. They threatened to sue Rick for not meeting his duty to use their parents' assets properly.

A court action had been filed to confirm Rick's authority as successor trustee, and Jake and Marta could not afford an attorney. This made them even more bitter and angry, and the wrangling continued. The parents were aware of the persistent wrangling, and it caused them both deep distress. Then the father died. The matter was finally resolved when their mother had to go to a nursing home, with cash assets depleted. The result was a breakdown of all the relationships in the family, caused by both the history of polarization between the two sets of siblings and also by the attorney's failure to ever explore the possibility of resolving the matter in a way that could have brought greater peace of mind to aging parents in failing health.

Skills You Need: Interviewing a Prospective Client About a Family-Related Dispute

Arguing families are difficult and stressful for the lawyer, regardless of which side of a case you find yourself handling. It is prudent to size up the matter thoroughly before stepping into the fray or initiating an action. People in crisis sometimes believe that they'll pay anything, do anything, and stop at nothing to get what they want. It is up to the lawyer to demonstrate the skill of standing outside the conflict and analyzing the extent and possible effects of the client's request.

Listening

As I see it, the most important interviewing skill is that of listening, which unfortunately is not emphasized in our legal education. It may be more difficult than we realize to sit still, not interrupt, and not tell the client what to do or how it is supposed to be before we fully understand the problem.

As described earlier, listening to an aging person takes patience. The same patience is needed to fully ascertain a family issue and determine whether you can be valuable and helpful or not.

For some kinds of cases, there is a somewhat standard set of questions we might ask on intake or when first contacted by the client. In family disputes concerning elders, I do not think there is much to standardize. Every family is different, not only in the issues it brings to you, but also in its history and relationships. It is a challenge to sort out, from all the information presented, how you can be useful. Hearing each person fully and without rushing to get to a conclusion will be very helpful to you.

Reiterating and Adding Your Impressions

When we reiterate or give feedback about what we just heard, we are confirming with the client that we got it right. That helps anyone feel understood. For instance, a client tells us how her mother is losing track of her bills and had the utilities cut off because she forgot to pay for them. We say, "I'm hearing that your mother is not able to remember to pay her bills." When we add our impression, such as "This must be a great worry for you that your mother is not able to manage her finances any longer," we are acknowledging that a client is stressed about it and that we understand that stress.

Asking Probing Questions

Of course, a client may not know what you want to find out about the presenting problem. You must ask questions. If there is a family conflict, you want to give the client an opening to tell you how the conflict started and how it got to the point where it is today. If the conflict is with an aging parent, you need information about the elder so you can figure out your next steps. Always ask if other family members are involved in the issue. You may learn a lot. Find out how the various family members get along. This information may not just surface on its own without you asking the right questions.

Ask About Others Who Have a Different Perspective

Sometimes it is very helpful to talk to other family members, assuming that they are not separately represented, to discover a point of view that may be different from your prospective client's view. It's a bit like interviewing witnesses, in that a case can take shape based on what the witnesses say without sole reliance on what the person currently before you is saying.

If an Elder's Competency Is an Issue, Ask About Medical Information

As we have discussed earlier, an elder's competency is frequently the point of contention in families or interwoven in the context of any related family dispute. In the illustration of Muriel's Case in Chapter 4, the lawyer representing her did not obtain threshold information about Muriel's diagnosis of dementia, which had been confirmed in a written report by a neuropsychologist. It had also been confirmed that Muriel was not able to safely make financial decisions independently. Nevertheless, her lawyer alleged that she was perfectly capable of making her own financial decisions. He later had to back away from that position, in view of medical evidence that was available well before he took the case. He ultimately agreed to have a professional fiduciary make financial decisions for Muriel. In this instance, the time, legal fees, and distress to the parties might well have been avoided had Muriel's attorney asked a few more probing questions. Had he gotten the reports before rushing into the case, it would have been better for his client, the elder, as well as her daughter and everyone else. Perhaps he was fooled by Muriel's "normal" social conversation with him. Again, I urge every lawyer to view an elder's self-reported information with caution. When an elder says "I'm fine," you may not get the whole picture.

Sibling Issues

Regardless of the combination of natural siblings, step-siblings, half-brothers and -sisters, adoptees, or other relationships, issues among siblings are a frequent source of distress in families with aging loved ones. These conflicts most often arise from the unplanned and unexpected. Families may not look ahead or ever discuss what could or should happen if parents need help in the future. They may never have contemplated the possibility of a parent's sudden or accidental demise when no one was ready to assume the parent's responsibilities. They may never have thought about a parent living into very old age, being disabled, or running out of money.

The following sections cover some commonly encountered areas giving rise to sibling conflicts. Any one of these or a combination thereof can drive the siblings to lawyers, looking to the lawyer to "make it right."

Shared Responsibility on Legal Documents

In my experience, it appears that critical decisions about which adult child will be in charge of a parent's health-care and finances are often emotionally driven. A parent may choose a child to take over the caregiver role based on liking one adult child more than another, or physical proximity to a particular child. The parent might choose to appoint a child who aligns with the parent's basic values or other preferences, rather than choosing the adult child who is actually best suited or qualified for the job.

The adult child who is most suited for the job may, in fact, be the one most likely to honor the wishes of the parent. Or not. These hidden factors can set the family up for conflicts when the elder becomes incapacitated and is no longer able to make independent or safe decisions.

When an incompetent adult child has been appointed as successor trustee, executor of the estate, or agent on a DPOA or health-care directive, there is still hope that families can work out the problem by agreement. Creative ways around the designations in documents do exist, and the best lawyers will come up with helpful suggestions rather than make a first strike at removing the apparently incompetent adult child. Family disagreements can quickly turn into lawsuits if no consideration is given to what impact the filing of a lawsuit will have on the relationships among siblings and the effect on the aging parent(s).

Particularly when the matriarch or patriarch is still living, the effect of sibling warfare on the parent can be very destructive. Even an elder with dementia is quite capable of experiencing distress and feeling emotion. If there is any way to spare them the pain of their children going at each other, it is worth the effort to consider it carefully.

Caregiving Issues

As we don't generally get lessons in how to care for aging relatives in school, many families are caught unprepared to take on the role of caregiver. It is unfamiliar. It can be thrust on adult children unexpectedly. Some 65.7 million caregivers make up 29 percent of the U.S. adult population providing care to someone who is ill, disabled, or aged.[1]

Many families are unprepared to face the legal, financial, emotional, and caregiving issues that their elders' increased longevity imposes upon them. When the money an elder has saved runs out because he or she has simply outlived it, it can create a myriad of difficulties for adult children and other relatives. The stress, increased responsibility, uneven sharing of duties, and the sheer workload lead to many a dispute.

How to Pay the Cost of Care

If the adult children find out that their elder is not eligible for any public benefit, and there is no way to pay for Mom or Dad's long-term care at home except out of pocket, they may turn on one another. For instance, an aging parent begins to demonstrate signs of memory loss, present in all forms of dementia. Mom can't live alone anymore. Or a parent falls, goes to the hospital, and is told that he can't return home because of reduced mobility after a hip fracture. Sometimes there is a crisis, such as a fire, the police being called into the home for some reason, or a diagnosis of life-threatening illness. These scenarios wake up the adult children to the frightening reality that no one planned for this, and there is no long-term

---

1. *The National Alliance for Caregiving and AARP (2009), Caregiving in the U.S. National Alliance for Caregiving,* Washington, D.C., updated: November 2012 (last accessed April 7, 2015).

care insurance. There is no ready source of funds for keeping a parent at home with caregivers.

The high cost of long-term care and our society's lack of public resources to pay for it create enormous stress in families. It may manifest in arguments and disputes over how to pay for care, who can afford it, who is "supposed to pay," and who is supposed to do other necessary tasks. Family warfare breaks out, masked as a legal issue that covers up fear of being saddled with responsibility for the cost of care.

What Is the Cost of Long-Term Care?

The Alzheimer's Association produces an annual report on dementia, which (among other things) tallies the cost of providing care in various settings. The figures are based on national data, averaged. The following information is taken from figures for 2011 in the 2013 *Alzheimer's Disease Facts and Figures* report. These apply to caring for an infirm person who needs help, whether the cause is dementia or another reason. The report comments that these figures are expected to rise over time.

- **Home Care:** A paid, nonlicensed caregiver coming into the home to help with things like bathing, shopping, meal preparation, walking, and other nonmedical needs averages $21 per hour or $168 per day nationally.
- **Adult Day Centers:** These are places that offer safety, supervision during the day, and activities for elders with health issues including dementia. The average cost of adult services was $70 per day. That amounts to $350 per week, or $17,640 per year. Some charge more for persons with dementia.
- **Assisted Living:** The average cost for basic services was $42,000 per year. Some facilities charge a different (higher) rate for people with memory loss or dementia. In those communities, the cost was $57,684 per year. The cost is higher in the more expensive places to live where apartment rents are higher than average for everyone.
- **Nursing Homes:** The average cost for a semi-private room in a nursing home was $222 per day, or $81,830 per year. It is higher in some parts

of the country. In California, for example, the average cost is $86,815, according to the *Genworth Cost of Care Study* for 2014.[2]

Most people prefer to stay in their own homes. Their adult children and those who provide advice to them may also share that goal. However, the average retiree does not have sufficient resources to pay the costs outlined above. This creates issues within families, which fight over who should pay for care, where the care will be delivered, and whether the family home should be sold to cover what is needed. If insufficient value in other assets is available to pay for care, families must take on the provision of care themselves. Many older adults are not financially prepared for long-term care at all. They have not discussed it with their families, and some have never done any financial planning for it.

How Lawyers Can Help

When you as a lawyer have aging clients and are preparing estate plans, it is essential to bring up the cost of long-term care with your clients. The details and facts of the high cost must be explored. "What would happen if . . . " conversations *must* take place. You can help your clients avoid considerable grief for their families by planning for all aspects of aging in advance, rather than just planning for what happens to an estate after a client's death. If it looks as if your client has limited assets other than the family home, a family discussion to explore how and where family could provide care is in order. If an elder must later depend on an adult child for every aspect of care, the lawyer can facilitate the family discussion, promoting enough communication about these issues to prevent family fights about things no one ever talked over before.

If you are a financial professional, it is critical to help educate your client about how much things can cost and how much she will need if she lives a long time and requires help, as most people do. If you believe that everything will be okay because an aging person who runs out of money

---

2. https://www.genworth.com/dam/Americas/US/PDFs/Consumer/corporate/130568_032514 _CostofCare_FINAL_nonsecure.pdf (last accessed March 12, 2015).

can get Medicaid and live in a nursing home, I offer you a personal perspective to the contrary.

I volunteered in a nursing home when I was in high school, feeding patients and reading to them. There was never enough staff. As a student nurse, I worked in nursing homes as an aide. There was never enough staff. They were grateful to get even a student nurse; at least we had sufficient training to properly care for our aging patients. I also worked per diem in a variety of nursing homes as an RN, both in a staff role and as a night supervisor. There was also sparse staff in those settings. I strongly suggest to you that living in a nursing home is not anyone's first choice. If there is anything you can do as a lawyer, planner, or advisor to protect a client from ending up there, *please do it.* I have sued nursing homes for abuse and neglect and I understand the dangers in these care facilities. Also, it is not as if assisted-living communities are all perfectly safe, either.

That said, I fully acknowledge that there are good nursing homes with good management and dedicated staff. I recently attended to a family member who was undergoing rehabilitation from a stroke in a nursing home. It was a well-run facility; things were very good . . . as long as I remained vigilant and insisted on being fully updated as to the care being rendered. If your client has the assets to provide for himself with long-term care, build in the expense of a professional care manager[3] as well. That help alone can do much to ensure a client's safety in receiving any long-term care.

As a professional, you can be a valued resource for your aging clients, guiding them to look ahead at the possibility or probability that they will need help. They most likely won't want to face these things, but it is part of your job to help them do so.

How to Handle an Elder's Escalating Needs

An adult child may start out helping an aging parent a few days a week. As the need increases, she may quit her job and move in to become a full-time caregiver. No one discusses whether or how the caregiving sibling should be compensated. Resentment over the increasing burden can grow.

---

3. Carolyn Rosenblatt, *The Family Guide to Aging Parents: Answers to Your Legal, Financial and Healthcare Questions* (Sanger, CA: Familius, 2015) .

Mistrust of a sibling who has moved in with a parent and has control over the parent's finances is as common as the burnout that so frequently occurs in the caregiver.

Because the emotional, physical, and financial burden on adult children who undertake caregiving duties can be heavy, stored resentment may surface after the fact. Not every family maintains open communication. Not every caregiver is honest about his or her response to unequal effort among siblings in helping an aging parent. Some suffer silently, and then feel entitled to an unequal share of the parent's estate after the parent passes away, regardless of what the estate documents say. They want to sue.

Many of the issues of caregiving have a significant legal component. Those legal issues, such as quantum meruit, contractual obligation, detrimental reliance, the right to live in a parent's home, the right to remove a parent from his or her own home, and so on, can come up, fester, spiral out of control, and eventually take the form of a lawsuit.

Unequal Sharing of Responsibility for Parents

Siblings who have aging, frail, and needy parents may not all be equally equipped to provide help. When some siblings are more financially secure and contribute to the support of parents, they may feel entitled to a greater share of the parents' estate, house, or other assets after the parents die. Others may be geographically closer and give more hands-on care than other siblings. The perceived or actual unfairnesses can create unrealistic expectations, slow-burning anger, and other conflicts among family members. All uneven contributions from siblings, either financial or personal, can create disputes either during the parents' last years or after they are gone.

Common Issues About the Right to Make Decisions

Who Should Handle Finances?

A decline in the elder's mental or physical health often brings into question who has the right to decide whether care is needed, and if so what kind, and where it will be given. It also raises the issue of who should be handling the elder's finances. A family trust may provide a clear means for a successor trustee to take over, or the language can pose burdensome and unrealistic conditions.

For example, I have seen trust documents specifying that a successor trustee may not succeed the settlor or original trustee unless the original trustee has been declared incompetent by a court. Imagine the expense of having to go to court to allow a successor trustee to assume the job of replacing an otherwise cooperative but impaired parent! We often encounter poorly drafted trust documents as a source of unfortunate family battles.

Other documents may state that the trustee must be declared incompetent to handle his or her own finances by a mental health provider, two doctors, or some other combination of doctors. Parents' trusts may have been drafted decades before the loss of capacity and never updated since. The original drafting attorney may be out of state or deceased by the time the issue arises for the family facing the trust and successor trustee question. We often see that there is no attorney currently involved in updating estate plans to accommodate changing conditions, such as a diagnosis of early dementia. At that time the elder may still have testamentary capacity to change the documents in anticipation of what is coming. Unfortunately, this is rarely done. The failure to look at the possible or likely long-term effects of diminishing financial capacity hangs over the family, rooted in the outdated and now unduly burdensome legal documents.

The elder may be unwilling to give up decision making, despite memory-loss problems, and refuse to voluntarily resign as trustee. Siblings may disagree about when the successor trustee should assume that role. There may be conflict about the person appointed as successor trustee or as agent on a durable power of attorney or health-care directive.

When Should the Successor Trustee Assume Responsibility?

A particularly thorny issue for those families whose aging parents have dementia and need to be replaced as trustees on the family trusts is that some aging parents refuse to see a doctor. Their adult children and sometimes their own spouses end up at odds with them.

Some individuals with dementia are in denial; others are actually so impaired that they do not know they have lost capacity. They say they are feeling fine, but it is obvious to all that their judgment is impaired. If this is your client, you will find yourself in an ethical dilemma. An impaired client is one who is vulnerable to financial abuse and who can decimate the family's finances. We hope that your lawyer's duty of loyalty will not blind you to the reality that if everyone else thinks the elder is impaired and no longer has financial capacity, maybe it's true. Maybe it's time to withdraw from representation if you cannot embrace the possibility that your client actually is impaired and must give up control over the family finances.

Disagreements About Competency of Aging Parents

Perhaps it is denial: No one wants to see a loved one decline in health and mental capacity, and few want to deal with this issue until they are absolutely forced to do so.

Disputes arise when one family member suddenly decides to get a parent or other elder to sign a new durable power of attorney, appointing that family member as agent over another sibling who was originally named. The same kind of issue arises when Mom or Dad, after having had an estate plan in place for years, goes to a new attorney at the urging of someone and changes the estate plan. Family warfare almost inevitably breaks out.

Regardless of the nature of the dispute about legal documents or an estate plan, no one wins when these disputes must be solved by litigation. Siblings against parents, siblings against each other, or stepparent/stepsibling polarization will inevitably be destructive. The question is why the "new attorney" failed to look into all the aspects of the proposed change to the estate plan, the DPOA, or other document. Changed plans that depart from long-held values and beliefs are a sure way to create family disputes. Suspicion as to motive arises and the conflict can quickly escalate.

Undue Influence

The issue of undue influence is a recurring one. The accusation of undue influence can come from anyone and be directed at anyone. We see lawyers, who are in a position to carefully consider how it will look to make late-in-life changes to an elder's legal documents, frequently fail to do so. Why do lawyers serving elders not look at the effect of the proposed legal work on both the elder and the family? No matter how vehement or urgent the request, there is an opportunity to step back long enough to explore whether the elder is being unduly influenced. Here is an example.

Illustration: Lola and Her Three Daughters

Lola is 89 and very frail. She has fallen several times at home, and was hospitalized and spent time in a rehabilitation facility after the last fall. Her husband, Mort, is her primary caregiver. Lola, who has dementia, is a quiet person who has always allowed her husband to make the decisions.

They have three adult daughters. Two have done well financially: Jeanine is a physician and Janet owns a business. The third daughter, Roseanne, struggles with money.

Lola had appointed her physician daughter, Jeanine, to hold her power of attorney and be her agent on the health-care directive. While Lola was in the rehab facility, Roseanne persuaded her to change the documents and name Roseanne as agent on the health-care directive and the durable power of attorney for finances. She then began to control when Jeanine and Janet could visit and limited their visits to an hour each.

Roseanne found an attorney and convinced her mother that she should get the attorney to change the trust, giving Roseanne a larger share of the inheritance because she was "doing more" for Lola when Lola needed her most. The lawyer did change the trust.

When Jeanine and Janet learned that Roseanne had persuaded Lola to change the trust, giving more to Roseanne, they were angry that she had pressured Lola into it. They could not learn more, as Roseanne would not allow Lola to discuss her estate with them. She insisted on being present when either Jeanine or Janet visited their mother.

Though Janet and Jeanine had never gotten along well with Roseanne, this change in legal documents was beyond anything they had ever expected. They were outraged. They decided to sue their sister. Roseanne had legal control and intended to seek conservatorship (guardianship) over her mother to secure her power over her sisters.

Money was not really an issue for either Jeanine or Janet. The issue was control. It so fractured this family that the sisters were left with no desire to reach compromise on anything. Lola felt the undercurrent of their distress and could not understand why Janet and Jeanine had to leave after just an hour visit.

In this situation, I question the lawyer who agreed to change the trust, knowing that the other two sisters could likely claim undue influence and manipulation of Lola for the benefit of Roseanne. What would you do?

Taking Away the Car Keys

The driving issue arises most frequently when siblings disagree about whether an aging parent is still safe to drive. It can also arise when the adult children are all in agreement that Mom or Dad should stop driving but the parent refuses to stop. When a parent has dementia, we know that his or her driving days are limited. In the middle stage of Alzheimer's disease, driving becomes problematic at best.[4]

Driving represents independence and control, two very highly charged and emotional areas. For elders in conflict with family members, the thought of giving up control may cause outrage, threats, fear, and other reactions the family is not prepared to address.

A dispute about the car keys can escalate into a legal battle: not just about driving, but about the larger issue of decision making. When lawyers are sought out, it is generally about more than just driving, as state motor vehicle departments can independently test an elder's driving ability. (There is no uniformity about this from state to state). Here is an example.

Illustration: Gallagher and the Driving Issue
Gallagher was 80 years old, and a very independent man, living alone. He had a teenage daughter by a second marriage late in life. He had been in poor health after his wife died, and felt lost. He wasn't doing well and was depressed.

His daughter moved into his house to look after him, against his wishes. When he was asleep one day, she decided he should not be driving and she hid his car keys. Gallagher was outraged. He promptly got another set made and went right to a lawyer to change his will to disinherit his daughter. She

---

4. P. Callone et al., *A Caregiver's Guide to Alzheimer's Disease* (Demos Medical Publishing 2006), 14.

returned fire with allegations that her father was incompetent and tried to get a guardianship over him. The expensive legal battle that ensued continued until Gallagher had a heart attack. At that point, the proceedings were suspended and eventually dismissed. Gallagher moved to assisted living and gave up driving on his own.

The lawyer who went along with the daughter apparently failed to look at the big picture, and failed to consider Gallagher's health as a factor in whether the contemplated action was a good idea. Gallagher was indeed competent enough that he was not going to be placed under guardianship, but he paid a stiff price—with his health—for the litigation.

Financial Abuse Accusations in Families

Allegations of elder abuse by one family member against another are not uncommon. Although a significant proportion of financial elder abuse is committed by financial institutions and professionals, most is committed by family members.[5] This is one area in which I do not see an alternative to reporting the abuse and litigating the allegations when sufficient evidence of abuse exists. Siblings who accuse another family member of abuse and are willing to report it and take legal action are in the minority; most cases go unreported.

If allegations of financial elder abuse are raised in a case in which you are involved, be sure to have all the facts and possible other perspectives in hand before taking an elder's word for it that he is or is not being financially abused. Sometimes the accusations are false. Sometimes the accuser is the abuser. Sometimes a lawyer can be fooled by a seemingly competent elder who is outraged about "abuse" when he has been unduly influenced to think that he is being abused when he is actually being manipulated. Here is a case in which I consulted with the victim of abuse, the family, and their legal representative.

---

5. National Committee for the Prevention of Elder Abuse, http://www.preventelderabuse.org /elderabuse/fin_abuse.html (2011) (last accessed March 12, 2015).

Illustration: Daniel's Father

Daniel and his brother Tom were at their wits' end with their father. Their dad still lived in the family home, but he had signs of early dementia. Their mother had died recently and she had made sure that Daniel not only had a durable power of attorney for the father, but also that the home had been put in Daniel's name, because Mom had been worried about their father's financial judgment.

Dad had been doing some strange things lately. He was approached by a couple offering to do "home repairs." They were scam artists. Two weeks later they were living in the house with Daniel's father and he was writing checks to them every week. He was not wealthy, and Daniel and Tom were very concerned. They hired a lawyer, who evicted the scammers. Two days later, they returned and Dad let them in. He believed they were his friends. Daniel had to tell his father that he was going to have to put him out of the house if the father did not get rid of the interlopers. Daniel also went to Dad's bank, warned them of the abuse, and asked them to honor the DPOA and not let Dad make withdrawals from his account.

Dad responded by hiring a lawyer. He told the lawyer that his son was financially abusing him and had blocked his bank account. The lawyer took Daniel's father to the bank, where he revoked the power of attorney; his lawyer told the bank teller that Dad was perfectly capable of deciding what he wanted to do with his own money and threatened to sue them if they tried to interfere.

You may ask yourself, what was Dad's lawyer thinking? Didn't he see that Dad was being financially abused? Did he even ask about Dad's tenants? Both had criminal convictions. Where were his own ethics? This is a real case, and this was the second lawyer Daniel's father had sought out. It was appalling to see the worsening of the risk to Daniel's father caused by his own lawyer's actions. Worse yet, Daniel was then forced to seek a guardianship over his father and probably had to evict his father from the house where he had lived for many years to get rid of the criminal tenant abusers. Daniel's father probably sounded quite normal in conversation with the lawyer he hired. However, that lawyer failed to look at the big picture, never talked to Daniel or Tom, and failed to protect the client from abuse by removing the only protection he had at the time: the durable power of attorney naming Daniel as agent. Do you think the lawyer would have acted differently if he had asked about anyone who might have a different perspective, or if he had inquired about the family history?

End-of-Life Issues

The impending loss of a parent brings up a host of family issues, and is a recurring source of conflict for many reasons. Our society does not easily undertake conversations about death and dying. We seem to have a peculiarly American prejudice against the subject, expressed in such common phrases as "in case anything ever happens to me." As if it might not!

Instead of directly talking with family about death, we avoid even the word itself and use vague, indirect language referring to "end of life." Consequently, siblings may find themselves facing immediate decisions about aging loved ones when discussion about what the elder wanted never took place.

When an elder suddenly falls ill, has an accident, or is diagnosed with a life-threatening illness, the family may be thrown into turmoil. Decisions must be made when an elder is not conscious and cannot speak for himself. Treating physicians and other caregivers want to know what the family wishes to do. Do they resuscitate a person whose heart stops? Do they institute artificial means to keep her breathing and hydrated? Do they insert a feeding tube? These are questions the family will be asked by health-care providers.

Every person in an elder's family may have a different view on the "right" action to take. Disagreements among family members may boil over into fights in the hospital corridor. The absence of a clear advance directive only fuels such disputes. A lawyer's best advice is to encourage every family member to *get the estate-planning documents in order*. Otherwise, we have no control over the sibling fight outside the dying parent's hospital room, which is almost sure to take place if no one has discussed end-of-life issues.

You have a choice about getting involved in the ugly hospital-family-sibling warfare concerning end-of-life issues, representing one against the other. However, be warned that the intense emotional content of these disputes will take a toll on the lawyer, as well as everyone else.

Prevention

One thing lawyers can to do prevent family fights about end-of-life decisions before it is too late is to seek the elderly client's permission to meet with the family members who would be in a position to make these decisions and to facilitate a discussion. The American Bar Association has excellent resources for families as well as for lawyers to use, particularly if we do not practice in the estate-planning field. For example, the toolkit for creating an advance health-care directive is very helpful, and I have used it with my own adult children. A lawyer can feel confident that downloading and encouraging an elder and family member to utilize these free resources can avert conflicts later in the elder's life.[6]

Hoarding and Other Intractable Problems

Some kinds of family conflicts are simply not amenable to legal resolution. Some problems do not even lend themselves to making agreements with the elder. These may be situations over which the elder does not have control or about which he or she cannot exercise reason or judgment.

Hoarding

Hoarding disorder is an example. Hoarding disorder[7] is a condition in which a person (the hoarder) forms an intense emotional attachment to collecting excessive amounts of objects or animals and is unable to discard them. This may be a manifestation of dementia or a separate pre existing problem.

It is entirely unlikely that a family will be able to get an aging parent who hoards to agree to clean up his home and remove the piles of excess objects, animals, purchases, or the like, as this particular problem is not one that yields to reason, arguments, or threats. It is not realistic to expect that a legal solution, other than guardianship, can be reached. Nor is it likely

---

6. "Consumer's Toolkit for Health Care Advance Planning," http://www.americanbar.org /groups/law_aging/resources/health_care_decision_making/consumer_s_toolkit_for_health _care_advance_planning.html (last accessed March 12, 2015).
7. "Diseases and Conditions: Hoarding Disorder," http: www.mayoclinic.com/health/hoarding /DS00966 (last accessed March 12, 2015).

that the affected elder could adhere to any agreement to cease hoarding. Even if guardianship is granted for reasons of health and safety, the hoarder will likely find a way to continue to hoard in a new environment, as this is an illness rather than a rational choice.

Mental Health Issues

Mental health issues affect our entire population, with about one in four adults suffering from a diagnosable mental disorder in a given year.[8] These problems do not magically lessen or disappear as we age. If an aging person has always struggled with mental health, the entire family is affected and will continue to be affected as the family member ages.

You will likely eventually meet some individuals with mental health problems in your practice, if you have not done so already. They may seem obviously impaired, or the problems may be more subtle and you hear about it from their adult children or caregivers. I mention them here because sometimes mental health problems are overlooked until they complicate any other legal work you may be doing with an elder.

Sometimes an elder's mental health difficulties can be successfully managed with referral to an appropriate care provider in your area. Sometimes they cannot be helped because of denial or refusal to seek or accept help. Because aging causes many losses and life transitions, elders are at risk for depression and other mental health difficulties. Imagine the loss of a spouse, friends, relatives. Imagine how losing your independence would feel. Imagine having to give up your dignity to accept physical help when you have trouble even seeing yourself that way. I believe it is prudent and useful for every lawyer to at least be aware of community resources and mental health providers so that you can offer a client or family member a direction if they want to take it. This does not mean that you become anyone's social worker. It merely means that you take the time to educate yourself about what private (as well as low-cost) mental health providers exist in the area where you serve your clients. The chances are that you will see an elder about some other legal business and realize that she can't seem to

---

8. R. C. Kessler, W. T. Chiu, O. Demler, & E. E. Walters, "Prevalence, Severity, and Comorbidity of Twelve-Month DSM-IV Disorders in the National Comorbidity Survey Replication (NCS-R)," *Archives of General Psychiatry, 62*(6), 617–627 (June 2005).

follow through on anything because she is mired in grief, or coping with a devastating diagnosis, or has undergone a trauma. That is the time to show your human side, recognize the suffering you see, and suggest with utmost respect that perhaps the person would benefit from some help. There is no harm in doing so; you do not have to follow up and ensure that the elder goes and gets the help. But not even acknowledging a mental health issue in front of you does not serve your client; your dismissal of the issue may stem from your own discomfort or other unpleasant emotion it brings up within you. If you want to work with elders, it is most helpful to get past your personal discomfort and see if you can suggest a resource to help your client.

I can only encourage you to become conversant with who the best elder psychologists and psychiatrists are in your area, and to have a list of some names to provide to those whose problems are obvious enough for you to notice. It is in a way equivalent to referring an elder to a lawyer who has an area of expertise different from your own. Mental health is an area outside your own expertise, so you serve your client by making a referral.

Substance Abuse

Substance abuse in elders is a somewhat hidden problem. Families focus on elders' physical disabilities, need for treatment for illnesses, financial problems, and caregiving issues. Behind the scenes, and in the course of addressing these other needs, many an adult child has confided in me that "Mom's been a drinker for years" or that "Dad puts away a six-pack of beer a day." What a lawyer needs to know is that alcohol abuse complicates a lot of the other issues facing elders—but there is little or nothing family can do about it. Likewise, we as lawyers can only recognize substance abuse and empathize with family members who have this additional complication in their lives. I see it as an intractable problem. There are a few exceptions, but elders with long-standing substance abuse issues are unlikely to seek or accept treatment. If they are in the habit of self-medicating emotional pain or other issues with alcohol, giving up this dependence would necessitate learning a very different way of coping. That is a challenge at any age and the effort to give up substance abuse has a high failure rate.

What we do need to deal with is the fact that alcohol abuse increases the risk for many other health problems. Heavy alcohol use may increase the risk of developing dementia, for example.[9] For clients with this issue, the need for advance planning about paying for long-term care increases dramatically.

General Perspectives in Working with Adult Families

The decision-making process among family members is rarely objective. Other agendas are often present, and these influence the perception of what should be done. When birth order, ego, personality, past resentment or mistrust, and relationship with the parent are all involved, families have difficulty seeing the big picture. Lack of objectivity in the family directly affects the ability of adult children to mobilize their creative resources to make decisions about Mom, Dad, or their own roles.

Some adult children may be aware of these hidden agendas, but most of the time they are just immersed in their own feelings. They may be locked in the past. Even when adult children are willing to directly acknowledge how past hurts and resentments color their ability to make decisions, they may still be unable to free themselves from their own prejudices about their family members. They may not be able to get past distrust, anxiety, and fear without competent advice from a skilled lawyer who *is* able to maintain objectivity.

There may be no one else in their lives who can or will point out what the lawyer, working to achieve a broader perspective of sibling conflict, sees. We are trained to spot issues and to analyze situations to solve problems. Families of elders and siblings in conflict will challenge this ability.

For readers of this chapter who are not lawyers, some of the same advice here applies to you as well. As a trusted professional who has a relationship with your client over time, consider having your own list of vetted other professionals outside your skill area to whom you can refer your clients when the needs described above present themselves to you. If you do not know any resources in your area, it is time to seek them out so that you

---

9. "Diseases and Conditions: Dementia," http://www.mayoclinic.org/diseases-conditions/dementia/basics/risk-factors/con-20034399 (last accessed March 12, 2015).

can offer them to aging clients, as they seem to need someone other than you to address their complex problems. Your local Area Agency on Aging, present in every county, is a good place to start. It may be available through your local Health and Human Services Department, which is the recipient of funding for these services.

Area Agencies on Aging (AAA) were originally funded by the federal government's Older Americans Act. These organizations coordinate a complex local service delivery system that serves millions of older adults and caregivers in every community in the country, providing access to critical home and community-based services, information and referral, and connection to professionals available to assist persons of every income level. Even if you personally do not know where else to refer an aging client or family member for help you cannot provide, you can refer to your AAA. To connect to your local AAA, call 800-677-1116 or find the closest one to your client service area online.[10]

Conclusion

Elders who present a problem for lawyers to solve often come with a large package of family issues attached to the problem. The complexity of the problems that elders present is magnified by their other family members, who often have varying agendas, different perspectives, and their own dysfunctional relationships.

Seeking to understand the family issues will help us to provide the best service to elders. Ignoring family issues can easily lead to disaster, as some of the illustrations in this chapter have shown us. A lawyer's patience, willingness to explore the big picture, and determination to gather information behind the presenting problem will permit the most reasoned and professional approach possible for resolving these problems.

---

10. www.n4a.org/olderamericansact (last accessed April 7, 2015)

6

Using Mediation for Family Disputes About Elders

Introduction

Most lawyers understand the use of mediation for legal cases. Lawyers are taught about mediation in law school. If they are litigators, they are often required to initially try some form of mediation to get their cases settled. Many lawyers themselves also serve as mediators. But apparently only a few consider using mediation for disputes involving elders before any case is filed in court. The concept of dispute resolution for elder-related matters, even with cases already filed in the courts, does not really seem to have caught on as yet.

Probate matters are an exception: Many are resolved, just as other kinds of cases are resolved, through alternative dispute resolution (ADR). The family conflicts that surface at the time a probate matter is disputed almost always have their roots in earlier conflicts. Those can sometimes be addressed much earlier in the legal process, before the matriarch or patriarch dies, and avert the worst probate battles. When mediation is not used or is not successful in a probate or will contest, the outcome is not likely to be satisfying for anyone. Probate litigation often consumes thousands of dollars of family assets on battles that leave everyone embittered, angry, and dissatisfied with the outcome. I believe that much more flexibility and creativity are available to lawyers and the family members they represent if mediation is used early in the process of any such dispute.

For nonlawyers, the concept of mediation may seem a bit vague. We see a labor dispute discussed on television, and there is mention of a mediator being brought in. The public, in general, may think mediation is for divorces, if it happens to be mandatory in one's state, or for worker contract conflicts—and that's it. Mediation is much more. This chapter presents many of the reasons why mediation can work for family disputes involving elders and why any person Working with Aging Clients should be aware of what it can do and how it can help. My purpose is not only to remind you, the reader, about what mediation does, but also to encourage you to think about it more often as a way to resolve some of the worst family battles you will ever see.

I believe mediation is an underutilized resource when it comes to conflicts about elders and involving elders. Everyone who works with an older client has the potential to witness a brewing or full-blown dispute about the elder or his property. Should that happen to you, this chapter can help you understand why mediation is valuable; it then details how you can suggest mediation, find a mediator, and encourage the use of mediation as an alternative to litigation. It can be a part of your proactive strategy to manage conflicts that you see coming.

Here we discuss the kinds of elder disputes that are suitable for mediation and, in fact, cannot be satisfactorily resolved without it. While it is true that some conflicts are not going to be settled with mediation, most can be resolved with this process, saving time, grief, distress, and money for all.

What Is Mediation?

Mediation is a voluntary process in which a neutral person outside the dispute is brought in to assist the parties to work out a solution to their conflict. The mediator must be neutral and can have no stake in the outcome. The mediator who serves best in this area will have good working knowledge of the issues that most elders may face and have excellent communication skills.

Mediation requires a meeting of some kind, usually face-to-face, to help the parties define what they want to work on and decide together what to do to unwind the conflict and move it toward resolution. The parties have to agree to go to mediation rather than being forced to do so. Generally, mediation is successful in resolving disputes about 80 percent of the time.[1] Those are good odds.

For those who are nonlawyer professionals, it is important to be clear about the difference between mediation and arbitration. Arbitration is a proceeding that typically takes place outside the courts, but it has some features in common with a case heard in court. In arbitration, an arbitrator, acting in the capacity of a judge, decides the outcome of a dispute. The opponents in an arbitrated matter may file their case in court or not, depending on the kind of dispute they have. There is a hearing at which the arbitrator listens to evidence, hears witness testimony, considers the papers that the parties present, and then decides the outcome for the parties.

Mediation, in contrast, does not have a "judge" deciding the outcome of the dispute. The mediator does not decide who is right or wrong or who wins. Instead, the mediator helps the parties to fashion their own outcome by the choices they make of ways to work things out. The mediator offers suggestions, gives information, and guides the discussion, making sure that all those present have a chance to talk and express their own points of view. The mediator asks helpful questions and assists those who are willing to compromise to see things from the other party's point of view. The mediator is a sort of coach, referee, and go-between, rather than a person who makes decisions for anyone else.

Family Involvement

Most conflicts about elders involve their families. Whether it is the elder who is the cause of conflict or it is a war among or between siblings, these fights are extremely stressful for all involved. Blood relationships and those created by marriage are some of the most emotional possible. In Working with Aging Clients, lawyers and other professionals are well served to keep in mind that a client's family is a critical part of solving many of the problems elders face. Seniors need the support, help, and involvement of their relatives. Some relatives are unprepared, unwilling, or incapable of giving

---

1. The Edwards Group Consultants, LLC, http://www.mediate.com/tegci/pg1.cfm (last accessed March 12, 2015).

the needed help. The uneven nature of who does what and who gives help is a source of conflict in many elder-related situations.

Besides lawyers, those who deal with aging clients as business advisors, accountants, brokers, real estate professionals, and others will inevitably witness all or part of conflicts affecting these clients. The distress associated with family conflicts spills over into other aspects of the elder's life and can affect all of the elder's business and professional dealings.

Family Battleground Issues

When aging clients show signs of diminishing capacity, it puts an additional burden on the professionals and service providers who help them, as the question of loss of decision-making capacity may affect any transaction the elder wants to undertake. Questions about competency are a frequent source of distress to the elder, and sometimes are the basis of family disputes.

Additional issues that frequently arise in families concern financial control, who will care for the aging person, who will pay for care, and failure by some families to plan ahead for a vulnerable loved one. Sometimes the source of conflict is a family member who was never able to "make it" on his own, and whose parents provided for him into adulthood. When the parents can no longer provide, because of their own disabilities or needs, other family members may want to change things, and this can lead to ugly confrontations. An example of this is the case of Ben.

Illustration: Ben's Support Structure
"Ben" was a middle-aged man who had not had a steady job in years. His parents took him back into their home after he was unable to support himself as a young man. He lived with his parents for years, offering little help with daily expenses. Simply put, he lived off of their generosity. This arrangement continued for decades until Ben's father died. His mother's health began to decline at the same time. Ben was not particularly well suited for the caregiver role. He had some mental health issues of his own, which probably accounted for his lack of success in the work world. Ben's siblings had to place their mother in a care facility after she was diagnosed with dementia.

The family home was the only asset, and it had to be sold to pay for the mother's care. This meant that Ben would be without a roof over his head and lacking support. The need to finance the mother's care in this way led to a long battle involving the siblings, three lawyers, and the expenditure of some of the equity in the home. An eviction proceeding against Ben was pending. By the time mediation was suggested, it was close to a trial date. It was too late to work things out for this family.

How might this very-high-expense battle have been avoided?

After Ben's father died, the family, at the urging of the estate-planning attorney, probate attorney, or any other professional who was aware of the family situation, could have suggested mediation. A problem-solving discussion or series of discussions could have enabled the family to decide what alternatives existed for Ben, other than having to force him out of the house and have him become homeless. Although the siblings were not a very functional group, it would not have been impossible for them to work on solutions and make agreements together.

A skilled and knowledgeable mediator could have offered numerous suggestions to this family. Everyone wanted a peaceful outcome, but no one could figure out how to achieve it. Ironically, one of the siblings was a lawyer, who was in a position to use his skill to refer Ben or help him to apply for various public benefits, but this was not done.

This destructive conflict, with the lawsuits, family arguments, eviction case, and legal fees that all occurred after the death of the patriarch, did not necessarily have to go the way it did. This case illustrates that waiting until a court date is set before even thinking of mediating a dispute may be too late.

The Impact of Longevity

Although people are living longer than ever before in this country, few seem well prepared for the financial, physical, and mental implications of that longevity. Most of us decline physically in advanced age, and often someone needs to help the older person with daily matters, whether it be care, chores, or finances. Elders may not be able to pay the high costs of such care. Their adult children must then step up, with either money or caregiving or both, and this puts unexpected pressure on them. Resentment may arise when one sibling takes on the caregiver role while others remain less involved or altogether uninvolved. Fights break out. Long-buried resentments resurface. Siblings who haven't spoken in years are forced to come together to make critical decisions about their parents or grand-parents. It can be very difficult to reach agreements and get things done under these circumstances.

A consistent problem I see as a result of people living longer than they thought they would is that they run out of money and assets to support themselves. A Social Security check, together with an average person's very modest pension, is often not enough to support an aging person. When they have to pay for the kind of care that Medicare does not cover—the so-called "custodial care" that most need—they do not have the funds to do so. This creates pressure on family members to either take in the elder, pay for the elder's care, or find a way to give the needed help. If the family does not have the assets to pay for care from hired caregivers, they may end up providing the needed help themselves.

Financial Pressure

When there are no or inadequate financial resources to cover care, some adult children quit their jobs, losing salary, retirement, and other benefits, to assume responsibility for the care of an aging parent, as there is no alterna-tive. If there are other siblings, this sacrifice by one child may lead to intense resentment and anger over the lack of fairness of the arrangement. Many a family conflict results when one sibling does more work than the others and silently fumes until things boil over or blow up into a fight down the road.

Can these disputes be avoided or helped by mediation? I believe they can. It does take forward thinking and preventive action by the professionals in the lives of the family members to suggest mediation of such incipient disputes. If the family is willing to meet with a mediator to work out a fair plan of caregiving before any sibling takes on caregiving responsibilities, the likelihood of a battle later on is greatly reduced.

Illustration: Trish and Her Brothers

Trish was a divorced, middle-aged mother of two sons who were in col-lege. She had a full-time job and was saving for her retirement. About a year after her mother passed away, Trish's father began to wander away from home and get lost. He also would forget to eat and was losing a lot of weight. Trish and her two brothers were deeply concerned. Her father's doctor warned that their father should not live alone anymore.

Of the siblings, Trish lived the closest to her father. He was a lot of work to take care of, but she decided to bring him into her modest home. This involved a lot of adjustment on her part, including paying a neighbor to watch him while she was at work. She eventually had to quit work to take care of him full-time. Her father owned a home, which was rented out to help pay for his basic needs.

Trish never said very much about the finances to her brothers, who visited rarely and did not offer any relief for Trish in the caregiving work. When she asked for help, they told her they were too busy. She was very angry at them.

After Trish's dad passed away, she felt entitled to a significantly larger share of the estate and the home than her brothers. The parents' trust stated that the estate assets were to be divided equally among the three siblings. She was very upset at this. She hired a lawyer, as did her brothers, and the fight was on.

Could mediation have prevented this dispute from becoming a court battle? I believe it might have. The time to seek mediation was at the point when their father was identified as needing full-time care. The brothers apparently expected Trish to take the job of caregiver without seeing that all of them could share in that responsibility in some way. A more equitable deal for her might well have been worked out in mediation ahead of the increasing burden of caregiving she took on and later came to resent.

A competent mediator might have encouraged the three siblings to seek legal advice and have a caregiver contract drawn up. Mediation could have helped them make decisions about the value of Trish's services to her father, which she alone bore. The brothers, if asked, might have been able to contribute money, relief caregiving, or other help so that the work and expense did not fall so disproportionately on Trish. Mediation could have been the place to determine the terms of a caregiver contract so that Trish would either get some financial compensation for caregiving or a larger share of the estate, or some other arrangement that would have recognized the value of her work and having to quit her job. All of these items could have been the subject of mediation so that anger did not build up over the entire time Trish cared for her father. When the anger surfaced in legal action, Trish became invested in the battle, and her brothers became invested in defeating her efforts.

Mediation in this situation would have given Trish and her brothers a good opportunity to recognize the problem, devise solutions that they could agree on, and have a plan in place to prevent a fight after their father died. A probate dispute, such as the one that they inadvertently set up by failure to communicate and use mediation, was costly, emotionally wrenching, and destructive of relationships.

Although mediation is a classic way of resolving disagreements, it is not likely to be the first method suggested when it comes to family disputes about elders. For lawyers who are representing one family member against another, litigation can pay quite well. Emotions among warring family members can be intense, and that alone can drive a conflict for months or even years. An unwillingness to suggest early mediation could be heightened by the fact that when a dispute is resolved and the case is settled, the litigating attorney's paycheck ends. Settling the dispute may be the best solution for the client, but it may not be the best economic outcome for the lawyer.

Exercising Professional Leadership

I suggest that attorneys who encounter such family disputes consider very closely what might be the best outcome in the shortest time for the client. That takes leadership by the attorney, of course. A client may not think of the option of mediation until the representing lawyer suggests it. Many lay people are not even aware that mediation is an option that might resolve their conflict without litigation. In the 27 years I spent as a litigator working with hundreds of clients, I do not recall a single client ever suggesting mediation in any matter. It was always up to the lawyers to bring up the subject.

Lawyers may also become aware of family disputes well before anything escalates to the point of one party filing a lawsuit against the other. Even if a lawsuit is filed, suggesting alternative dispute resolution early can be effective. Early mediation is ideal, as the conflict is present but none of the parties have yet "dug in" and spent a lot of money on it; it is generally easier to resolve a dispute before the parties become heavily invested.

Lawyers are normally in a position of influence with their clients and can promote the use of mediation, even over client doubts and objections. That is most fair to the client and upholds the lawyer's ethical duty of loyalty to the client. While it is true that not every client is willing to listen to such advice, the lawyer who suggests mediation has an excellent opportunity to educate the client about its benefits. Most clients want to save money, time, and aggravation, and mediation offers a way to do just that, so this is an excellent persuasion point.

Other professionals, whether in financial services, accounting, or other business relationships with clients, also have an opportunity to suggest a peaceful way for a client to resolve a family disagreement, rather than simply sitting passively by and listening to the reasons for the dispute. Anyone can suggest mediation. Mediators are available though local bar association directories as well as through an Internet search, using sites such as Mediate.com. While it may be more difficult to find a mediator who focuses on elder disputes, it is possible to find a good mediator who has the necessary skills to be of help. I urge those working with elders to consider this, even if you have never done so before. The purpose of this book is to help raise your awareness of how to give the best service to your aging clients. One way to render good service is to offer a suggestion to help a client understand that he has the mediation option when disputes come up.

What Makes a Good Mediator for Disputes Involving Elders?

I recently heard the saying that "technique can be taught but talent cannot." As an elder mediator myself, I believe that saying applies to mediators as much as anyone else. Anyone who wants to take mediation training can learn mediation techniques. However, working with families is a special area of mediation: One must have a desire to do it and a feel for it. The emotional content of any mediation can be quite high, whether it is a business disagreement, an injury case, an employment matter, or another kind of case. However, it is hard to imagine any kind of dispute more fraught with intense emotion than a family battle, whether the elder is living or has passed away. An elder mediator must be willing to deal with the intensity of emotion involved and must have a good sense of how to address it. Some of this can be taught. I believe, though, that some people are simply better prepared emotionally to manage this intensity gracefully when serving as a neutral elder mediator. Mediators who are drawn to and interested in elder-related matters may hold themselves out as doing this particular kind of mediation; it becomes their specialty.

Basic Training

As a start, any mediator should have undergone the basics of mediation training. Forty hours of instruction and practice in doing "mock mediations" is generally considered the minimum. An elder mediator should also have an interest in working with families and an appreciation of what makes working with an aging client different from working with a younger one.

Many mediators are lawyers, and because family dynamics is not taught in law school, I believe that you must look very carefully at the background and experience of the lawyer-mediator if you are seeking an elder mediator. A person with a background or experience in social work, health-care, psychology, or family counseling would have a definite advantage, as these disciplines require education and training in working with families. However, these kinds of training do not guarantee that the individual will also be adept at conflict resolution, which requires a separate skill set. I have met lawyer-mediators who have no background in family dynamics who are nonetheless able to work well with families. Likewise, having a relevant background is no guarantee of a compatible mediator for an elder-related dispute. Finding a good elder mediator is much like finding a competent professional for anything else you need: you have to do your research, ask for recommendations from those you trust, and get a feel for the mediator's personality and style through a phone or in-person conversation.

Critical Skills

Above all, the mediator should demonstrate an excellent ability to listen and skill in guiding the disputing parties toward resolution. That takes more than just listening while the parties rant about their anger, vent other emotions, or repeat their basis for the disagreement. It takes a sense of when to step in, when to offer information and suggestions, and when to urge consideration of the other party's point of view. The best mediators have good success with most disputes and will likely have a good reputation. Those are the ones to seek for help with your client's dispute. Being a great litigator or even a retired judge does not ensure that a person will automatically have great mediator skills. During my career as a litigator, I personally met plenty of retired judges who were not particularly good at mediation. They were more accustomed to making decisive rulings from the bench than helping all the parties to feel heard. They did not all have the ability to persuade a party to reconsider a position and to give up a stubbornly held position in order to reach a settlement. The ability to elicit a willingness to change and compromise one's stance is an intangible, but one you should look for in a mediator. If you hear about it when you check out a mediator's reputation, you're on the right track in getting someone to help your client with an elder-related dispute. Successful mediators offer what is probably as much art (talent) as it is good technique.

Besides being comfortable in working with family dynamics, it is helpful if the mediator has a solid grounding in the problems that elders face in our society. One must be familiar with these problems to be effective. A qualified mediator needs to be able to make suggestions when families get stuck on a problem or a point. For example, if siblings disagree about whether it is safe for their aging parent to remain in the home independently, the elder mediator might suggest that the family get an objective evaluation of the elder from a geriatric care manager.[2] If the mediator has no idea that this resource exists, she will be less capable of offering useful suggestions.

As elder disputes, particularly in probate and estate matters, often involve the family home or other real estate, knowledge of real estate transactions is also helpful background. Skills that include understanding of health-care resources, dementia, and other frequently encountered problems affecting elders can also add to the value and ability of an elder mediator. These are a few examples of how a mediator's general knowledge can contribute to the progress and success of a mediation. Educating the participants about

---

2. Carolyn Rosenblatt, *The Boomer's Guide to Aging Parents*, Vol. 5, "How to Find and Use a Care Manager," (Amazon, 2008), 25.

what information is available to them and how to get it can do much to move a dispute toward resolution.

Depending on the complexity of the dispute and the number of parties involved, mediation of elder matters can take place over a session or two—or a mediation may require numerous sessions. The mediator must be able to stay with it for the long haul when necessary.

Personal Qualities

I enumerate here only a few of the essential mediator qualities that lead to successful outcomes; there are many. Mediators are in the business of making peace when possible. Their ability to actively listen, to be willing to engage with the parties in conflict and to hear their points of view without judging anyone is crucial and probably primary. If the parties to the conflict trust the mediator, they are much more likely to listen to suggestions. They may be willing to take direction about considering opposing points of view if they are comfortable with the mediator.

The ability to meet with relative strangers and quickly establish a trusting relationship, which we sometimes call *rapport*, is another essential mediator quality.

Yet another essential quality is the ability to persuade the parties to change their positions. A successful mediation invariably involves compromise. Someone has to give up something to reach resolution. Usually everyone has to give up a lot to reach an agreement. The mediator has to be able to convince each party to look at the overall dispute from the other person's viewpoint and recognize how changing his or her beliefs and demands can lead to settling the matter. This can be very difficult at the best of times, and is even more so when emotions are running high. A skilled mediator is able to help the parties reach common ground by using a combination of experience, skill, talent, persuasion, and technique to get to the result everyone wants: an end to the fight.

Willingness to Confront the Heart of Conflict

Most people prefer not to take on conflict, and want to avoid the inevitably unpleasant part of confrontation with others. All of us have experienced conflict at some point in our lives and have learned how painful it is. We don't want to repeat painful experiences, so we shy away from conflict. A mediator, however, must be willing to get involved with the most unpleasant, sad, emotional, wrenching things people say and do to one another during conflict. This job is not for the faint of heart.

Illustration: The Scylla Sisters

I offer this example of high conflict in a mediation I handled involving two sisters locked in battle over their deceased father's estate. They were both exceptionally distrustful of each other and had been battling for seven years over their father's home and financial accounts. The police had been involved in locking one sister out of the home. Bitter accusations and name-calling constantly flew back and forth. Many thousands of dollars had already been spent on lawyers, and three new lawyers had been involved over time. The lawyers were unable to make any headway. Each had a hard time controlling his client. An eviction proceeding was pending, as was another part of the case in a different court.

Mediation first took place for a two-hour period at the court, which required that all eviction matters be mediated. We were able to establish a working relationship during that time, despite the nasty words traded by the litigants and the lawyers' basically futile efforts to keep a lid on the fray. Tears were shed. Emotional outbursts took place. Accusations of fault continued. It was not a pleasant scene.

The parties agreed to meet for a half-day mediation soon after. When they came together, ground rules were established. No name calling was one of them. No interrupting was another. There was a great deal of resistance at first, but eventually the two sisters began to find common ground, and we began to make headway. After two more sessions, the battle was nearly over. The home was to be sold and agreements were reached on most areas of dispute. A written settlement agreement was signed. A seven-year court struggle was brought to a close.

My willingness to be totally involved with the conflict and to engage fully with the parties was essential to the successful outcome, as it would be for any mediator in any mediation. Using mediation works well when the parties cannot talk to each other without having it deteriorate into a verbal battle and being sidetracked by old history and resentments. The mediator acts as somewhat of a referee, helping the lawyers control the parties and themselves when the lawyers have previously been unable to reach resolution.

This case also serves as an example of how a family fight over the patriarch's estate could well have dissipated most or all of the estate assets. The sisters were not going to give up their opposing positions, even though they knew that they were rapidly spending their remaining inheritance in fighting with one another.

Working with Two Mediators

The practice of having more than one mediator is generally followed in community mediations, health-care mediations, and other settings. In courts offering litigants help with settling their cases shortly before trial, the practice often includes using two experienced lawyers to act as a panel to help the litigants work on settlement. Although a court-sponsored settlement conference is not technically a mediation because it is not voluntary, it does share many features with mediation. When co-panelists each offer the parties suggestions, direction, and opinions, their collective input can do more than one settlement panelist alone could do.

Likewise, co-mediation in an elder dispute can be extremely valuable in getting matters resolved. I believe that a mediator who has skill in dealing with mental health issues is an exceptionally useful resource.

The Benefits of Having Two Mediators

Two mediators can offer complementary approaches to the parties, thus reinforcing the effectiveness of the process. Two mediators can appeal to different individuals in different ways. Where one mediator is limited to a single perspective and experience, the use of two mediators doubles the breadth of problem-solving abilities.

My business partner and husband is a clinical psychologist who has decades of experience in working with families. When I began my mediation practice, I asked him to join me and become my co-mediator. He had not done mediation before and did not have formal mediation training, but he agreed to try it. One of our courts had already developed an innovative program to bring mental health professionals into its settlement panels for family law matters, and this court wanted to expand the program to other kinds of cases. It offered a half-day training for mental health professionals to assist with case settlements. He took the training and found that he was in familiar territory. Many of the skills a mediator uses are those a psychologist or other mental health provider uses as well. Listening well is foremost among them.

Here, however, I must distinguish mediation of family disputes from family therapy. These are very different processes. The purpose of mediation is to resolve a conflict, to reach agreements, and to address a specific presenting problem—sometimes defined through a lawsuit, and sometimes not. Mediation is generally *not* directed toward the broader goal of creating better relationships, though reaching agreements can improve relationships. It also has a different time frame. Generally, there is at least one session, and some cases are resolved in a single session. It may take several mediation sessions to get a matter resolved, but except in very complex, multi party cases, the process typically does not require weekly meetings over a long period of time, as therapy usually does. An example of the kind of mediation that requires months to resolve would be a corporate business dispute with layers of difficulty and numerous lawyers.

The outcome of a successful mediation is resolution of a dispute between or among parties. It can be a settlement that results in one party paying money damages to another party, or it may be a different way of reaching resolution through agreement.

Psychotherapy, in contrast, is directed at correcting maladaptive behaviors, changing distorted thinking patterns, and improving relationships with self and others. It may include treating psychological disorders and illnesses. It is longer-term than mediation and has a much broader reach and intent. It may have other purposes as well.

The time frame too is different, as regular, one-on-one sessions are the norm. In working with families, therapists may meet with the group many times to sort out the problems in interpersonal relationships. The desired outcome is self-improvement or improvement in decision making that is part of relationships.

How a Mental Health Professional Can Help a Mediation

From our own court-sponsored program to bring mental health professionals into the settlement process, we have seen great success and learned some valuable lessons. Psychologists and other mental health professionals improve outcomes in mediation by adding their unique skills. Psychologists see beyond the realm of reason and logic better than lawyer-mediators often do. They quickly discern how best to respond to the emotional content the parties express or (importantly) emotions the parties seem unable to express. That is what appears to drive most of the family conflicts I observe: the emotions of the parties.

Mental health professionals, by training, are highly skilled listeners. They seek to understand the emotional needs behind the parties' words. Once the emotional content is articulated by the mediator, the parties are much more likely to feel acknowledged and understood. As most mediators clearly understand, helping the parties to feel acknowledged and understood is fundamental to getting them closer to making agreements. Additionally, once the emotional underpinnings of the conflict are brought to the fore, the motivation for the fight is often radically reduced.

For a lawyer representing an aging client or the family beneficiaries of an estate who are battling with one another, it is likely that the right mental health professional can add a great deal to the prospects for success in mediation. In short, sometimes it's not just about the money, even though that is how the parties characterize the dispute. It is often really about other, deeper issues, and it can be very helpful to dig out and address the ones that may be getting in the way of resolution. The dimension of psychological expertise, when added to the help of someone whose training prepares her fully to help any mediator, can be invaluable with the most difficult and intense family disputes.

Mental Health Issues in Working with Elders and Their Families

I have the good fortune of having an "in-house" mental health professional to work with me in consulting with families and in mediating family disputes. My business partner and husband, Dr. Mikol Davis, is a clinical psychologist with 40 years of experience in the field. What we have observed in our mediation and consulting practice while working with elders and their families is a significant incidence of mental health issues in the families we serve. This problem is not limited to mediation: Mental health issues pervade many family disputes and cases that never get to mediation. But in mediation, it is particularly difficult to reach resolution of any dispute when one or more of the parties presents with a significant mental health problem. In fact, from personal observation, I can state that the mental health issue of one or more of those involved in the dispute is often at the very root of the dispute.

Mental illnesses are common in the United States. According to the National Institutes of Health, in 2012 there were an estimated 43.7 million adults aged 18 or older in the United States with some kind of mental illness during the prior year. This represented 18.6 percent of all U.S. adults.[3]

What this means is that when you work with families and elders, whether separately or together, on family disputes, you are likely to encounter someone with a mental health problem. It is not something you can ignore. If you observe signs leading you to believe that your client, opponent, client family member, or another professional involved in the dispute has a mental health problem, you will be well served to seek a mediator who is willing and able to include a co-mediator who is a mental health professional.

From personal experience, I know that you will be glad to have a skilled mental health person in the room when you are trying to work on agreements with someone who is exceptionally difficult. Sometimes a person's conduct is so unreasonable, you think you'll never get anywhere in trying to get a case or conflict resolved, and you may just run out of ideas as to how to work with that difficult person. It has happened to me—but when Dr. Davis, my co-mediator, knew just what to say to get her back at the bargaining table after she threatened to walk out, I was greatly relieved. We did eventually reach a settlement agreement in that matter.

I encourage lawyers and other professionals to get to know experienced psychologists, counselors, and qualified others to assist you in solving the

---

3. National Institute of Mental Health, "Any Mental Illness (AMI) Among Adults," http://www .nimh.nih.gov/health/statistics/prevalence/any-mental-illness-ami-among-adults.shtml, last accessed March 12, 2015).

problems you will face when mental health issues are a part of the elder's family picture.

The Role of Lawyers and Other Professionals Working with Difficult Families

If you are trying to accomplish a task or transaction with an elder and the family is part of a problem you are having, you may wish that the family would get family therapy. Family disputes can interfere with any business at hand that affects family members. Therapy could perhaps take the matter out of your hands. However, having a family fix all its internal problems is not essential to getting your work done. Sometimes dysfunctional family members who need to move a matter forward and who are unwilling to go to family therapy are willing to go to mediation. That is your opportunity to make use of mediation to facilitate your own work goals. In any legal or business matter, reducing the conflict in order to create an atmosphere of better cooperation can help the lawyer or business professional meet the challenge of completing the work at hand. The most important message to take from this is to keep mediation in mind for any elder and family who appear to be stuck in their disagreements. You may be instrumental in bringing up the idea of mediation.

Estates and Trusts: Other Common Battleground Issues

Besides finances and care of an elder while the elder is still living, there are many issues with the estates of elders that come up after the elder's passing. Trustee battles are unfortunately common, as many trustees are unprepared for the complexity that is thrust upon them in administering an estate. They may have been appointed by a well-meaning parent who saw that individual as likely to succeed in the job of trustee, but the responsibility can be extremely difficult for an inexperienced person to handle well. Research has shown that when wealth is transferred, the control over the family assets fails about 70 percent of the time.[4]

---

4. Roy Williams & Vic Preisser, *Preparing Heirs: Five Steps to Successful Transition of Family Wealth and Values* (San Francisco: Robert D. Reed Publishers 2003), 17.

Unprepared and unqualified trustees raise the anger and distress of the other beneficiaries of the family trust, and fights break out. Lawsuits are often the result. Failure among families to prepare for transition and breakdown of trust and communication are the key components in failed wealth transfers.[5]

This suggests that when a lawyer who may be advising the family about the family business, or real estate management, or other matters sees family communication issues, she needs to address the communication problem if she wants to be effective. Proactively mediating such conflicts can help. The same is true for any financial professional, accountant, tax consultant, or other professional who wants the family to succeed. You alone may do your job very well, but if the elder and his family are always fighting about something, the full effect of your good work can be lost.

While some families may need more than mediation to really work in depth on their underlying conflicts, using mediation can help re-establish trust in critical ways, piece by piece. The making of even one agreement can lead distrustful people to get along better, just as a result of succeeding at something that required cooperation. That can serve as a catalyst to creating other agreements.

I refer once again to the case of the Scylla sisters, set out earlier. They would have been well served by going to mediation much earlier than they did. If things had continued on the same path as they were headed when the case first came to my attention, they could have spent all of the available cash in their trust on attorney's fees, accountants to check other accountants' work, appraisers, and so on. This could have been an illustration of how a wealth transfer failed, even though the patriarch had done good estate-planning. The investment advice was sound, as the assets had survived the test of time and the ups and downs of the market. The lawyers were making their best efforts to be good advocates. They were representing their clients well. But the sisters' failure to learn how to reach agreements was a crucial and dangerously destructive element in the overall picture. Did they need family therapy? Of course. Their underlying mistrust went back to their childhood. However,

---

5. *Id.*, 31.

through mediation they were able to reach resolution of major disputes about trustee accounting, distribution of cash assets, and the value of the family home.

Finding a Mediator for Elder Disputes

Mediators can be found in all major cities, particularly through bar associations, as many mediators are lawyers. However, a law degree is not necessary for becoming a mediator, and some excellent mediators are not lawyers. Some list themselves on the Internet as private mediators and some work through organizations of mediators. At the end of this book, I list some resources to use in finding a mediator who has expertise in elder-related matters. Elder mediators are probably harder to find than those who do not specialize in this area, as elder mediation is a relatively new area. As I have stated, it also seems to be much underutilized. If you are looking for a mediator and cannot find one who calls himself an elder mediator, look for one with experience in the area of family law, probate and estate matters, or family issues. There is a significant resemblance between family law issues over support, money, division of assets, and decision making and the issues in elder mediation. In my own experience, a good mediator with a talent for getting to the heart of a conflict and handling emotional matters will be a good bet for nearly any kind of dispute. That could include elder mediation as well. However, the intensity of family disputes is not for every mediator. Lack of experience in the subject matter outlined in the earlier chapters of this book would also be a disadvantage. However, I believe that anyone who really wants to get a dispute resolved through mediation can find a competent mediator to help. If you are that person, when looking for a good mediator, do what you would do to find any helpful professional: ask those you know for recommendations and do your research to check out the person(s) suggested to you.

Conclusion

Family disputes are perhaps an inevitable part of working with elders and their families. If we are to be effective in preventing these conflicts from spinning out of control, which they can easily do, we have to think proactively.

The lawyer or other professional alone may not be able to get the business at hand done, because family disputes can destroy working relationships and prevent the kinds of agreements needed in the ordinary work we do. We need to consider mediation as a way of resolving disputes before they escalate to the lawsuit and court level.

I hope that with the information in this chapter, you may remember and suggest the use of mediation more often. For those of you who have not thought about it for your clients, bring it up, encourage it, and see how well it can work for you. It can reduce stress, not only in your client's life, but in yours as well. Peacemaking through mediation is different from therapy, and it is important not to confuse the two. Even a client who would *never* go to therapy, no matter how much he might need it, might be willing to try mediation as a way of reaching important agreements in any kind of dispute. When you as a professional exercise leadership by suggesting and encouraging mediation of elder disputes, you are likely to experience greater success in resolving them.

Resources

Publications

Becker, Ernest, *The Denial of Death* (New York:
Free Press Paperbacks, 1997).

Birkel, Richard, Lauran Granberry, & Gayle Alston.
"Evidence-Based Practices and the Rosalynn Carter
Institute," *Generations, Journal of the American
Society on Aging, 34*(1), 13–18 (Spring 2010).

Callone, P., C. Kudlacek & B. Basiloff. *A Caregiver's
Guide to Alzheimer's Disease* (New York:
Demos Medical Publishing, 2003).

Derocher, Robert J. "Licensing Older Drivers: Renewed Calls for
In-Person Testing." *Experience, 18*(2), 13–16 (Winter 2008).

Ghatak, Rita, PhD. "A Unique Support Model for Dementia
Patients and Their Families in a Tertiary Hospital
Setting: Description and Preliminary Data," *Clinical
Gerontologist, 34*(2), 160–164 (March-April 2011).

Gillick, Muriel R., MD. *The Denial of Aging: Perpetual
Youth, External Life and Other Dangerous Fantasies*
(Cambridge: Harvard University Press, 2006).

Johnson, Vernon E. *Intervention: How to Help Someone Who Doesn't
Want Help* (Minneapolis: Johnson Institute Books, 1986).

Lebow, Grace, & Barbara Kane. *Coping with Your
Difficult Older Parent: A Guide for Stressed-
Out Children* (New York: Quill, 2002).

Mace, Nancy L., MA & Peter Rabins, MD, MPH. *The 36-Hour
Day: A Family Guide to Caring for Persons with Alzheimer
Disease, Related Dementing Illnesses, and Memory Loss in
Later Life* (3d ed.) (John Hopkins University Press, 1999).

Meckelson, Doug & Diane Haithman. *The Elder Wisdom Circle: Guide for Meaningful Life* (Plume/Penguin Group, 2007).
Rosenblatt, Carolyn, *The Family Guide to Aging Parents* (Sanger, Cal.: Familius, 2015).
Taylor, Dan. *The Parent Care Conversation* (New York: Penguin, 2006).

Websites

General Information
Administration on Aging: http://www.aoa.gov
Alzheimer's Association: http://www.alz.org
National Association of Area Agencies on Aging: http://www.n4a.org
National Family Caregivers Association, Caregiver Action Network: http://www.nfcacares.org; http://www.caregiveraction.org/
Safe Driving
AAA Foundation for Traffic Safety: http://www.aaafoundation.org
AAA Roadwise Review: https://www.aaafoundation.org/roadwise-review-online
AARP Driver Safety: http://www.aarp.org/home-garden/transportation/driver_safety/?intcmp=HP-LN-INFO-DSP
American Medical Association's *Physician's Guide to Assessing and Counseling Older Drivers*: http://www.nhtsa.gov/people/injury/olddrive/OlderDriversBook/pages/Contents.html
American Occupational Therapy Association: http://www.aota.org/olderdriver
Aging Parents and Adult Children
Aging Parents and Legal, Caregiver, Family Issues : http://www.AgingParents.com
Aging Parents Forbes blog, Carolyn Rosenblatt : http://www.forbes.com/sites/carolynrosenblatt
The Family Security Planner: https://xl168.infusionsoft.com/app/manageCart/addProduct?productId=3

Elders Finances and Financial Advisor—Investment
   Issues: http://AgingInvestor.com
eBook: *How to Talk to Your Aging Parents About Finances:*
   https://xl168.infusionsoft.com/app/manageCart
   /addProduct?productID=37

To Find a Mediator

http://www.aarp.org/home-family/caregiving/info-04-2012
   /how-to-choose-an-elder-mediator.html
http://www.eldercaremediators.com
http://www.mediate.com